EASY to BUILD
backyard
PROJECTS

EASY to BUILD
backyard
PROJECTS

Monte Burch

CRE▲TIVE
HOMEOWNER®
CREATIVE HOMEOWNER®, Upper Saddle River, New Jersey

Easy-to-Build Backyard Projects was produced for
Creative Homeowner by Moseley Road Rights & Packaging,
129 Main Street, Irvington, NY 10533
www.moseleyroad.com

EASY-TO-BUILD BACKYARD PROJECTS
SENIOR EDITOR Suzanne Lander
ART DIRECTORS Gus Yoo, Brian MacMullen
DESIGN AND LAYOUT Gus Yoo
JUNIOR EDITOR Rachael Lanicci
PHOTO COORDINATOR Ben DeWalt
FRONT COVER DESIGN Gus Yoo

CREATIVE HOMEOWNER

VICE PRESIDENT AND PUBLISHER Timothy O. Bakke
ART DIRECTOR David Geer
MANAGING EDITOR Fran J. Donegan

Current Printing (last digit)
2 4 6 8 10 9 7 5 3

Printed in China

ISBN: 978-1-59258-301-0

CRE▲TIVE
HOMEOWNER®

A Division of Federal Marketing Corp.
24 Park Way
Upper Saddle River, NJ 07458
www.creativehomeowner.com

SAFETY

Although the methods in this book have been reviewed for safety, it is not possible to overstate the importance of using the safest methods you can. What follows are reminders—some do's and don'ts of work safety—to use along with your common sense

■ Always use caution, care, and good judgment when following the procedures described in this book.

■ Always be sure that the electrical setup is safe, that no circuit is overloaded, and that all power tools and outlets are properly grounded. Do not use power tools in wet locations.

■ Always read container labels on paints, solvents, and other products; provide ventilation; and observe all other warnings.

■ Always read the manufacturer's instructions for using a tool, especially the warnings.

■ Use hold-downs and push sticks whenever possible when working on a table saw. Avoid working short pieces if you can.

■ Always remove the key from any drill chuck (portable or press) before starting the drill.

■ Always pay deliberate attention to how a tool works so that you can avoid being injured.

■ Always know the limitations of your tools. Do not try to force them to do what they were not designed to do.

■ Always make sure that any adjustment is locked before proceeding. For example, always check the rip fence on a table saw or the bevel adjustment on a portable saw before starting to work.

■ Always clamp small pieces to a bench or other work surface when using a power tool.

■ Always wear the appropriate rubber gloves when handling chemicals, moving or stacking limber, working with concrete, or doing heavy construction.

■ Always wear a disposable face mask when you create dust by sawing or sanding. Use a special filtering respirator when working with toxic substances and solvents.

■ Never work with power tools when your are tired or when under the influence of alcohol or drugs.

■ Never work while wearing loose clothing, open cuffs, or jewelry; tie back long hair.

■ Always wear eye protection, especially when using power tools or striking metal on metal or concrete; a chip can fly off, for example, when chiseling concrete.

■ Always be aware that there is seldom enough time for your body's reflexes to save you from injury from a power tool in a dangerous situation; everything happens too fast. Be alert!

■ Always keep your hands away from the business ends of blades, cutters, and bits.

■ Always hold a circular saw firmly, usually with both hands.

■ Always use a drill with an auxiliary handle to control the torque when using large-size bits.

■ Always check your local building codes when planning new construction. The codes are intended to protect public safety and should be observed to the letter.

■ Never cut tiny pieces of wood or pipe using a power saw. When you need a small piece, saw it from a securely clamped longer piece.

■ Never change a saw blade or a drill or router bit unless the power cord is unplugged. Do not depend on the switch being off. You might accidentally hit it.

■ Never work in insufficient lighting.

■ Never work with dull tools. Have them sharpened, or learn how to sharpen them yourself.

■ Never use a power tool on a workpiece—large or small—that is not firmly supported.

■ Never saw a workpiece that spans a large distance between horses without close support on each side of the cut; the piece can bend, closing on and jamming the blade, causing saw kickback.

■ When sawing, never support a workpiece from underneath with your leg or other part of your body.

■ Never carry sharp or pointed tools, such as utility knives, awls, or chisels, in your pocket. If you want to carry any of these tools, use a special-purpose tool belt that has leather pockets and holders.

CONTENTS

Introduction

THE PROJECTS

Chapter 1: Seating

Chapter 2: Outdoor Cooking

Chapter 3: For Kids

Chapter 4: For Gardeners

Chapter 5: For Decks

Chapter 6: Around the Yard

RESOURCES

Introduction

Welcome to *Easy-to-Build Backyard Projects*!

When it comes to home construction, off-the-shelf lumber lies at the heart of the woodworking process. Your home has hundreds of 2x4s inside the walls, because they're dependable, easy to acquire, and efficient to use. Combined with other standard lumber, like 1x4s and utility plywood, 2x4s are the material of choice for the backbone of your home. For those same reasons, they're perfect for woodworking projects outside your home.

In the pages of *Easy-to-Build Backyard Projects*, you'll learn how to make beautiful chairs; handy accessories for the patio, deck, and barbecue grill; and pieces any gardener will love. You'll even make some great things for your kids—and, hopefully, you can share the building experience with them.

MATERIALS

The materials required for these projects are all standard-dimension lumber or plywood. Most common dimension lumber is pine or fir, which are also the most economical. These materials, however, do not weather well, and can rot or succumb to insects within a short time—especially if regularly exposed to weather. I once constructed a deck of common 2x6 pine boards **(Photo 1)**. I thought I was being economical, until I had to rebuild it within five years.

Two woods that are extremely weather- and insect-resistant include California redwood and western red cedar. Both these woods are more expensive than common pine or fir. They may not be available at some building supply dealers, but you can usually get them at larger traditional lumberyards. Both have a very attractive color and are great for projects where appearance is important. They are also softwoods and easy to work **(Photo 2)**.

According to the U.S. Forest Products Laboratory, redwood heartwood ranks among a limited number of American woods that are durable even when used under conditions that favor decay. Redwood has been successfully employed for exterior siding, tanks, hot tubs, and other exterior structures requiring a serviceable, long-lasting wood. Redwood also has a very low rate of shrinkage and swelling under a varying humidity levels. This prevents warping and splitting when used in exterior projects. Another feature of redwood is uniform texture and straight grain. Redwood also contains no pitch or resins and will readily take and retain paints and stains. Available in a number of grades, the most popular are clear all heart, clear, select heart, select, construction heart, construction, and merchantable. The number, size, and nature of knots and other characteristics (such as color) determine the grades. Construction heart, one of the more economical grades, does not contain sapwood and provides an excellent choice for these outdoor projects **(Photo 3)**. One of the main features of California redwood is its beautiful reddish color, and this can be enhanced with the proper exterior clear finishes. Left without a finish it eventually turns into a beautiful gray.

Western red cedar provides another excellent option. Slow growing and naturally durable, western red cedar has one of the longest life spans of any North American softwood, and it's resistance to decay rates as the wood's most valuable characteristic. Western red cedar fibers contain natural compounds called "thujaplicins" that act as natural preservatives. Free of pitch and resins, western red cedar will take a wide range of finishes. This wood also has great dimensional stability, and it's

Introduction

easy to cut and handle. This species, however, does have a corrosive effect on some unprotected metals, which can cause a black stain on the wood. All fasteners and metal in contact with the wood should be made of corrosion-resistant materials, such as aluminum, brass, or hot-dipped galvanized or stainless steel **(Photo 4)**.

Pressure-treated wood has become extremely popular for outdoor construction, including projects such as some in this book. Pressure-treated wood, including plywood and dimension lumber, is readily available at almost any building supply dealer and in all the most popular dimension lumber sizes. Pressure-treated wood is treated under pressure with preservatives. In the past, pressure-treated wood, called CCA, contained arsenic and was not safe for some projects. The newer "next generation" products, however, using copper azola and alkaline copper quaternary, is sold under a number of brand names. These new copper-protected woods look, last, and work much like the green-colored wood of the past. Some wood contains patented preservatives such as a formulation of copper azoles, along with organic azoles, to protect against copper-resistant fungi. When you purchase pressure-treated wood, it is still "green" from the treatment, and as it dries, it shrinks. This can cause some problems with cracking, splitting, and warping. Treated wood can be dried after treatment, preventing this problem. This is called redrying and is indicated on the end tag by ADAT (Air-Dried After Treatment) or KDAT (Kiln-Dried After Treatment). Drying makes the wood lighter in weight and ready for immediate painting or finishing. Not all wood treaters, however, offer redried products **(Photos 5 nd 6)**.

All fasteners, nails, screws and hardware should be for outdoor use and include galvanized or stainless-steel nails, and galvanized, brass, or stainless-steel screws. Screws used with pressure-treated wood must be classified as for use with pressure-treated wood. Some of these may not be readily available at the big-box stores, but getting them is worth the extra effort **(Photo 7)**.

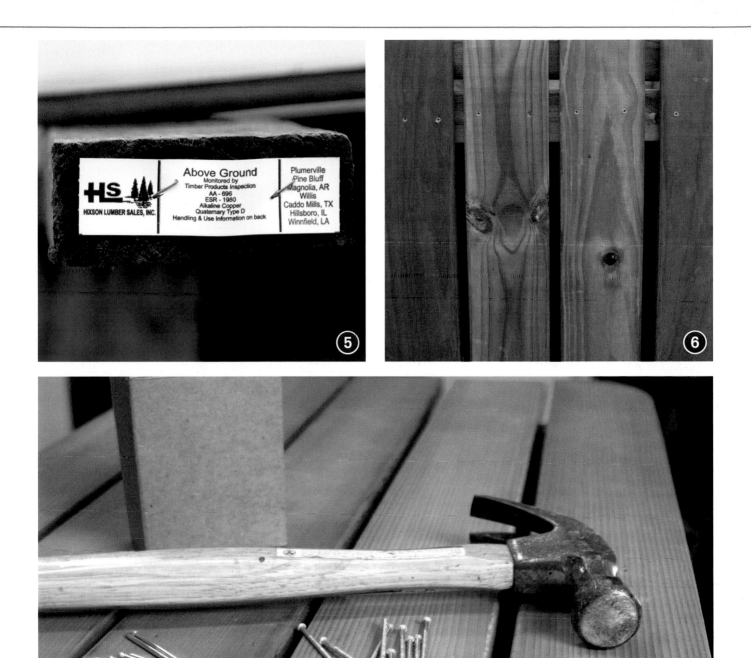

Introduction

(8)

to match existing backyard decor or to create accent pieces. Make sure you use an exterior latex paint. A number of clear or stain-coat oil sealants are also available for wood projects. These are available in clear or stain colors and can be applied by brush, roller, or spray.

For outdoor projects, one-coat wood finish comes in clear or "toned" colors. I especially like the cedar tone. An easy-to-apply, one-coat oil and alkyd resin formula provides protection from exposure to rain, sleet, and snow. It also provides a barrier against ultraviolet sun rays, providing further protection and longevity for the wood. Treated wood must be absolutely dry before the finish is applied.

LUMBER DIMENSIONS

A 2x4 is the most common example of *dimension lumber*, building material made up of various types of wooden boards with a system of standardized sizes. A woodworker can get a 2x4 at any home center or lumber company and be reasonably certain it will be the same size as one from any other.

Dimension lumber is available in a range of sizes; while the 2x4 is the most common, "2-by" lumber also comes in 2-, 6-, 8-, 10- and 12-inch widths. It's important to remember that the dimensions are nominal only—a 2x4 really measures 1½ x 3½. Other common dimension lumber includes "1-by" stock, measuring a nominal 1 inch thick (it's really ¾), with widths of 2, 3, 4, 6, 8, 10 and 12 inches. Finally, 4x4 lumber, 3½ x 3½-inch beams often used as posts, rounds out the field. One last type of dimension lumber should be mentioned: plywood. Coming in standard thicknesses of ¼, ½ and ¾ inch, plywood is sold in sheets that can be cut to any size.

The wood most often used for 2x4s and other dimension lumber is simple pine, but Douglas fir, oak, and poplar are also commonly available at home centers. Some centers may also carry maple and western red cedar.

The ready availability of dimension lumber, its reliable standardized sizes, and the general ease-of-use make it the perfect choice for outdoor projects. For that reason, you'll need nothing more to make all the projects in this book than what you'll find a short drive away, at your local home center.

From many years of constructing decks and outdoor projects, I have my favorite wood screws, which are self-starting. I find that they do not strip out as do most other screws when used with the more powerful drill/drivers. They are available for use with woods such as cedar or redwood and formulated for use with pressure-treated wood **(Photo 8)**.

In many instances the addition of glue can create stronger joints and longer-lasting projects. Choose the glue appropriate for your particular job, keeping in mind whether it will be exposed to the outdoors.

Many projects are simply allowed to weather without a finish. You may also wish to paint some projects

This chart shows the actual sizes of the various dimension lumbers.

LUMBER SIZES	
Off-the-shelf Name	Actual Dimension
1x2	3/4" x 1 1/2"
1x3	3/4" x 2 1/2"
1x4	3/4" x 3 1/2"
1x6	3/4" x 5 1/2"
1x8	3/4" x 7 1/4"
1x10	3/4" x 9 1/4"
1x12	3/4" x 11 1/4"
5/4x4	1" x 3 1/2"
5/4x6	1" x 5 1/2"
2x2	1 1/2" x 1 1/2"
2x4	1 1/2" x 3 1/2"
2x6	1 1/2" x 5 1/2"
2x8	1 1/2" x 7 1/4"
2x10	1 1/2" x 9 1/4"
2x12	1 1/2" x 11 1/4"
4x4	3 1/2" x 3 1/2"
4x6	3 1/2" x 5 1/2"
4x8	3 1/2" x 7 1/4"
6x6	5 1/2" x 5 1/2"

NAILS

Nails come in a variety of sizes and shapes. Not only is it important to use the proper nail, but the correct size as well. Nails are designated by the "penny" (abbreviated d). An 8d, or eight-penny nail, is about 2½ inches long, and a 10d nail is about 3 inches long. The most commonly used nails are 4d, 6d, 8d, 10d, and 16d. You more often use the latter in framing than in smaller projects. In the past, nails were commonly sold by the pound or in bulk, with the salesperson weighing out the amount needed. Today nails are more often sold already boxed.

NAIL SIZES	
Penny Size	Length
2d	1"
3d	1 1/4"
4d	1 1/2"
6d	2"
7d	2 1/4"
8d	2 1/2"
9d	2 3/4"
10d	3"
12d	3 1/4"

Nails are also available in different shapes. Common nails have a large flat head and are used where strength is needed and the exposed flat head doesn't cause a problem with the appearance of the project. Finishing nails have a smaller head that is often set slightly below the wood surface using a nail set. Uncoated, plain steel nails will rust, causing unsightly stains when exposed to the weather.

SAFETY

Working with tools, both hand and powered, requires careful attention to safety rules. Make sure you understand how to operate power tools, and carefully follow the manufacturer's safety instructions in the owner's manual. Make sure you keep all tools sharp and in good working order. Don't wear loose or floppy clothing and keep long hair tied safely back. Always wear safety glasses during all operations, especially cutting chores. Wear ear-plugs or hearing protectors when running power equipment. Wear a dust mask during

9

Introduction

INTRODUCTION

power tool cutting chores. When working with pressure-treated wood, make sure you wear a dust mask and safety gloves **(Photo 9)**.

TOOLS AND TECHNIQUES

All the projects in this book can be constructed with hand tools with the exception of cutting the curved portions. These can be cut with a hand coping saw, but it's a real hassle. You will need a handful of hand tools, including a tape measure, level, carpenter's square, a couple of wrenches, a chisel set, and a handsaw (the best choice is a toolbox model); a speed square can also make marking for cutting easy **(Photo 10)**. Clamps can help in holding parts for assembly. And you'll need sandpaper and paintbrushes. Two hammers can be useful, including a general purpose

framing hammer and a smaller 12-ounce finishing hammer **(Photo 11)**. You may also wish to have a miter box and miter saw if you don't wish to purchase a power miter saw **(Photo 12)**.

Power tools make the construction much simpler, and in many instances of first-timers, make better joints. Power tools maybe portable or stationary and are available in a wide range of sizes and prices. The more economical tools will do the chore quite easily, but the better tools will last longer, and once you experience the fun of woodworking from these projects, you'll probably want to tackle more projects in the future. Today, power tools are available in the traditional corded models, utilizing 120-volt power, or in cordless rechargeable models. The latter have become increasingly popular and are also available in a wide range of sizes, from 9- up to 36-volt (power), and prices. The

biggest difference in both power and cost is the type of batteries used. The newer lithium-ion batteries offer much more power with less weight **(Photo 13)**.

The most common and most used tool is a portable electric drill-driver. These and a set of bits can be used to drill holes, and then a driver bit used to drive screws. In most instances nails and screws should have holes predrilled before driving the fasteners **(Photo 14)**. Dedicated impact drivers can fasten screws faster and easier than drill/drivers, but are more costly **(Photo 15)**.

A portable circular saw not only speeds up cutting chores but creates more accurate cuts. For crosscuts, mark across the board using a speed square, and then follow the line with the saw shoe **(Photo 16)**. Stock can be cut along the grain using a portable electric saw with a ripping guide **(Photo 17)**. When cutting plywood, place it across 2x4 supports, and set the saw blade to just penetrate the plywood thickness **(Photo 18)** A saber saw is the best choice for making irregular cuts **(Photo 19)**.

An orbital sander can be used to sand and smooth

Introduction

(20)

edges and surfaces **(Photo 20)**. A router is used to rout moldings and create decorative edges **(Photo 21)**. One of the handiest tools is a power miter saw. The one shown is cordless, making it even handier **(Photo 22)**. You can set a power miter saw to cross-cut **(Photo 23)**. In addition, you can cut bevels across the stock **(Photo 24)**. This versatile saw can also cut angles for 45-degree miter joints **(Photo 25)**.

ENLARGING BY THE SQUARES

In lieu of full-size patterns, one method of creating patterns for irregularly shaped project pieces is with squared drawings. This allows small drawings of pat-

(21)

(22)

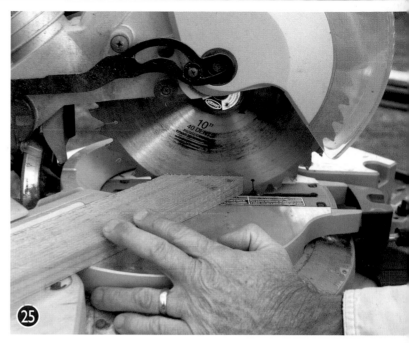

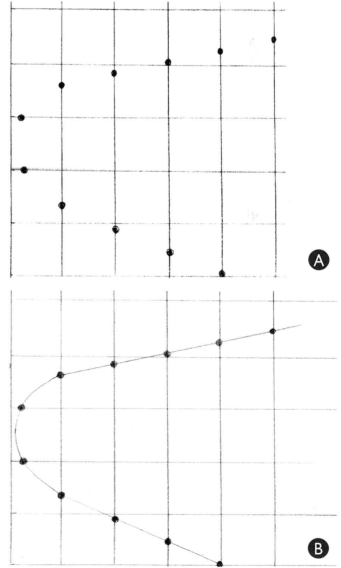

terns that will fit in the book. The patterns are drawn to scale and overlaid with a grid of squares. Shown is how to create a pattern for the Adirondack Stool legs.

Step 1. To create full-size patterns, first make up a grid of one-inch squares the size of the pattern. Then count the squares on the smaller drawings in the book and place dots where the pattern lines cross the lines of the one-inch squares on your grid **(Drawing A)**.

Step 2. Connect the dots; then round any curves to follow the pattern outline **(Drawing B)**.

The Projects

Time to Complete: 4-5 Hours

Adirondack Chair, Footstool, and Table

The traditional Adirondack chair could probably be called the original "lounge" chair. With its slatted bottom and slanted back, the chair has long provided pleasant seating for sun worshipers, and it's just as popular today. Add a footstool and you have comfortable seating for your deck, patio, porch, or yard. You might as well figure on making at least two while you're at it, because you're bound to have company. The chairs were typically constructed of pine, making them extremely economical to build, one of the reasons for their popularity, and painted white. The chair, footstool, and occasional table set shown, however, was made from California redwood and left as is to weather to a nice gray color. If the furniture is made of other, rot-prone lumber such as pine, it will need to be painted.

Adirondack Chair, Footstool, and Table

ADIRONDACK CHAIR

Shopping List:

1 2x4, 12' long

1 1x8, 10' long

2 1x4, 10' long

1 1x4, 6' long

1 1x6, 8' long

Stainless-steel nails and screws

Cutting List:

2 Front posts, 1½" x 3½" x 22"

1 Front seat support, 1½" x 3½" x 22"

1 Rear seat support, 1½" x 3½" x 22"

6 Seat slats, ¾" x 3½" x 23½"

2 legs ¾" x 7¼" x 32" (cut to length)

1 Upper back splat support, ¾" x 3½" x 22"

1 Center back splat, ¾" x 7¼" x 36"

2 Side back splats, ¾" x 3½" x 33"

2 Side back splats, ¾" x 3½" x 30"

2 Arms, ¾" x 5½" x 31"

1 Rear Arm support, 1½" x 3½" x 26"

2 Arm supports, 1½" x 3" x 3"

ADIRONDACK FOOTSTOOL

Shopping List:

1 2x4, 4' long

1 1x8, 6' long

1 1x4, 12' long

3" Stainless-steel nails and acrews

Cutting List:

2 Rear posts, 1½" x 3½" x 13¾"

2 Legs, ¾" x 7¼" x 24"

1 Rear slat support, 1½" x 3½" x 20½"

6 Slats, ¾" x 3½" x 22"

ADIRONDACK OCCASIONAL TABLE

Shopping List:

1 1x6, 10' long

2 1x4, 10' long

Stainless-steel nails and acrews

Cutting List:

8 Leg pieces, ¾" x 5½" x 13"

2 Aprons, ¾" x 3½" x 22"

2 Aprons, ¾" x 3½" x 16½"

5 Top pieces, ¾" x 3½" x 28"

Adirondack Chair

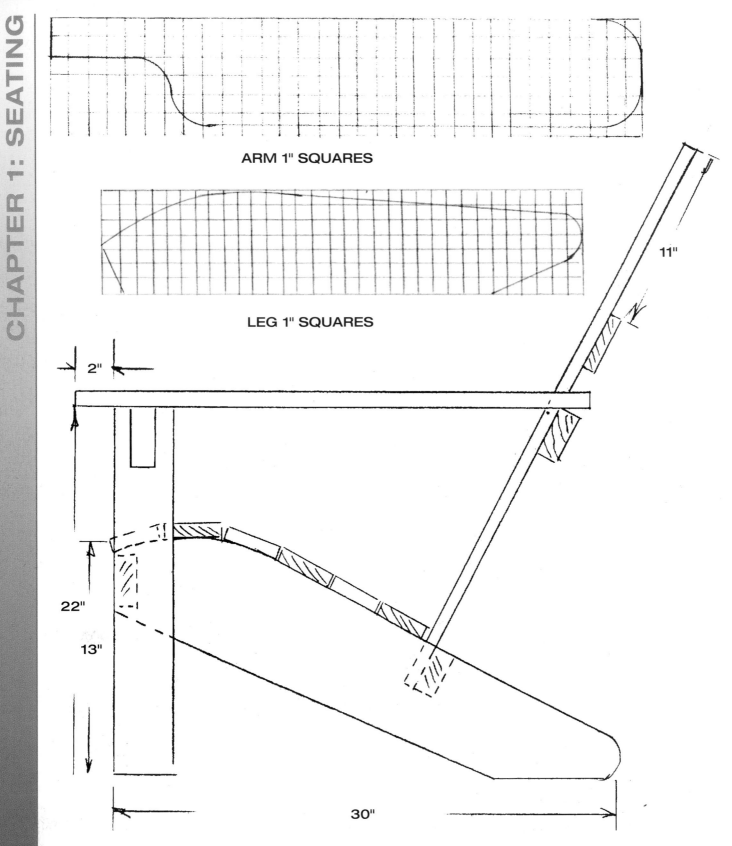

ARM 1" SQUARES

LEG 1" SQUARES

11"

2"

22"

13"

30"

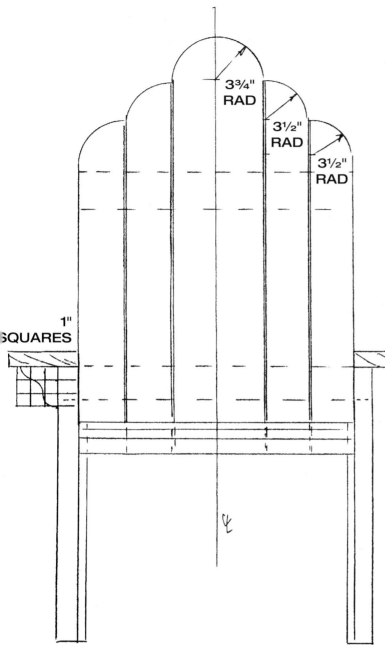

3¾"
RAD

3½"
RAD

3½"
RAD

1"
SQUARES

① ② ③

First step is to enlarge the square drawings for the legs, arms, arm braces, and back splats, and make a pattern for each **(Drawings)**. Trace the pattern onto the stock; then use a saber saw to cut the pieces to the correct shape **(Photo 1)**. Use a sander to sand all cut edges smooth. Cut the front and rear seat braces, and install them in place between the legs with stainless-steel screws. Note that you must predrill all holes. The front brace is installed using two screws. Temporarily install the rear brace with only one screw in each end at this time **(Photo 2)**.

Cut the seat slats to length, and install them in place with stainless or galvanized nails **(Photo 3)**. Cut the front posts, and fasten them to the outside of the front of the legs with

Adirondack Chair

④

screws through the legs and into the front seat-support board **(Photo 4)**.

Remove the rear seat board, and lay it as well as the upper back support on a smooth flat surface. Position the center back splat in the center of the rear seat-support board, and locate the upper back support. Using 1¼-inch stainless-steel screws, fasten the center splat using the screws. Then fasten the remaining seat slats in place, spacing them equally **(Photo 5)**.

Fasten the arms to the front posts with wood screws through the arms into the posts **(Photo 6)**. Fasten the arm supports to the arms and front posts **(Photo 7)**. Fasten the back splat support to the splats; then attach the rear arm support with screws through the splats, and fasten the back ends of the arms down on the support **(Photo 8)**.

⑤

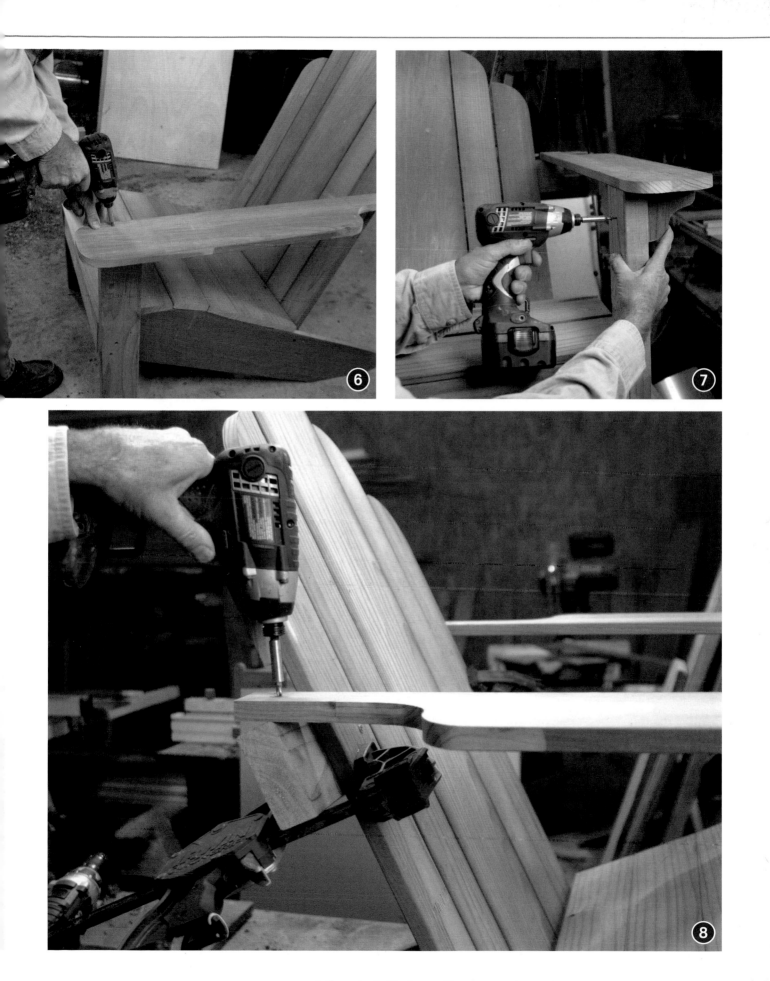

Adirondack Footstool

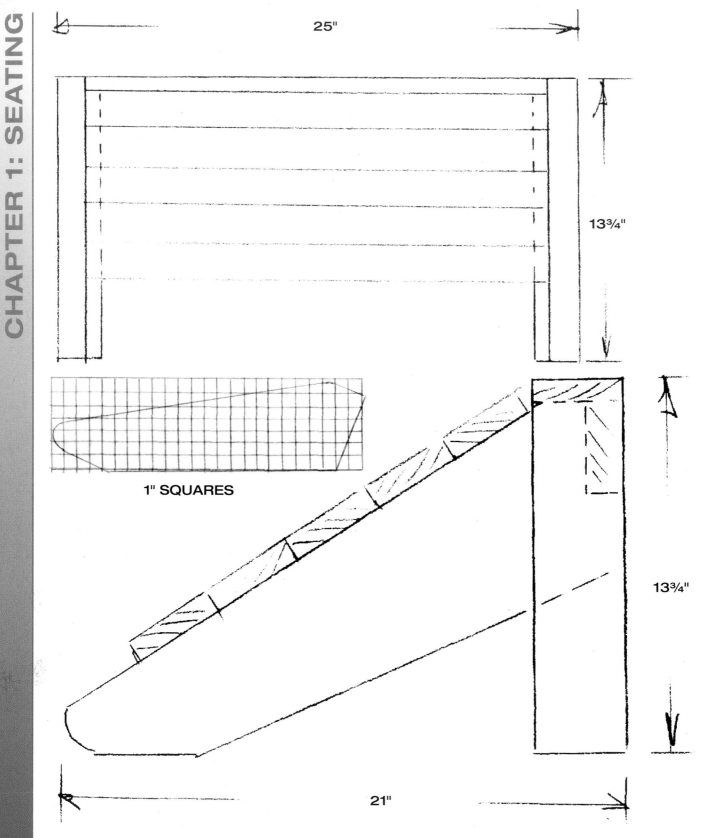

25"

13¾"

1" SQUARES

13¾"

21"

A matching footstool makes the Adirondack chair even more of a sun-lounger. Also made of redwood, the footstool is a very easy project to construct.

First step is to enlarge the squared drawing and make a pattern for the legs **(Drawings)**. Then using a saber saw, cut the legs to shape **(Photo 1)**. Sand all edges smooth.

Cut the rear support piece to length, and fasten the legs to it using screws. Cut the rear posts to length, and fasten to the side assembly, leaving ¾-inch protruding above the side assembly. Drive only one 3-inch screw in the upper end of each post into the leg assembly.

Sit the stool on a smooth, flat surface, and adjust the legs and posts until the stool sits flat and doesn't rock. It's almost impossible to make these patterns exact from the squared drawings, and you will have to make some adjustments. Once the stool sits flat, drive a second 3-inch screw in each post and into the assembly **(Photo 2)**.

Cut the seat slats to length, and fasten them down on the legs with stainless-steel or galvanized nails **(Photo 3)**.

Adirondack Occasional Table

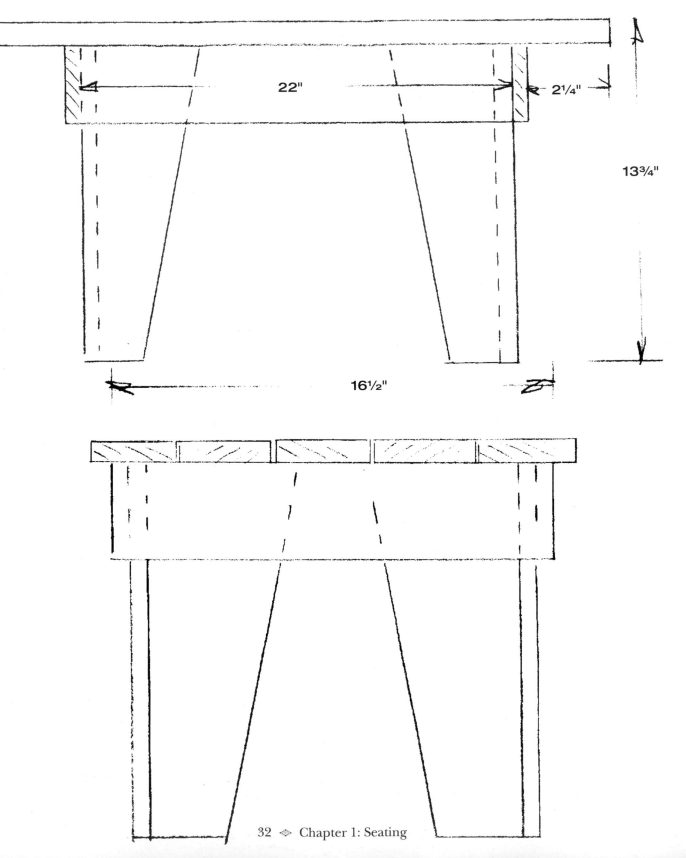

22"

2¼"

13¾"

16½"

Designed to match the Adirondack chair and footstool, this little table is quite simple to build and an elegant addition to the ensemble. With two chairs, footstools, and a table between, you have a great spot to relax with a friend or family member.

The table is made of California redwood in the same manner as the chair and footstool (**Drawings**). First step is to lay out the tapered leg pieces and cut them to shape using a saber saw (**Photo 1**). Fasten the leg pieces together (two sections per leg) using stainless-steel or galvanized nails. Predrill the holes for all fasteners to avoid splitting the wood (**Photo 2**).

Cut the aprons to length, and fasten the leg assemblies to the aprons using 1¼-inch screws or galvanized nails (**Photo 3**). Cut the top pieces to length. Use a compass to mark a rounded end on each end of the outer top pieces. Then cut the rounded corners using a saber saw (**Photo 4**). Sand the cut edges smooth.

Fasten the top pieces in place, starting with an outside piece, making sure they are positioned correctly (**Photo 5**). Use stainless-steel or galvanized nails.

Time to Complete: 4-5 Hours

Deck Rail Benches

Benches made of the same material to match your deck can help tie the design together. In this case, the deck was constructed of pressure-treated lumber. Attached to deck rails, benches create permanent seating areas. The rail and bench construction shown utilizes a slanted-back rail system and slightly angled seats, which provide a more comfortable backrest. In some instances the railings are attached to the deck supports, which extend through the deck. In this case, the railings are created separate from the deck and then fastened in place. This makes it easy to pre-assemble parts of the bench in the shop and then attach the parts to the deck. The railing and bench pieces should be given a coat of finish to match the deck before being attached to it. The railing benches can be as long as you like, even running the full length of the deck. You will need to provide a post-bench support for each end and for every 6 feet of bench.

DECK RAIL BENCHES

Shopping List:

1 2x6, 8' long

2 2x6, 12' long

3 2x4, 6' long

1 ⁵⁄₄x6, 6' long

3" deck screws suitable for pressure-treated lumber

2" deck screws suitable for pressure-treated lumber

4 ³⁄₈" x 6" lag bolts

Cutting List:

(for one 6-foot section)

Back braces, 1½" x 5½" x 45½"

2 Seat-board braces, 1½" x 3½" x 20"

2 Front legs, 1½" x 3½" x 16"

2 Bottom Braces, 1½" x 1½" x 18"

3 Seat Boards, 1½" x 5½" x 6'

1 Top Trim, 1" x 5½" x 6'

1 Upper Rail, 1½" x 3½" x 6'

1 Lower Rail, 1½" x 5½" x 6'

2 End Trim, 1½" x 1½" x 16½" (cut to fit)

Deck Rail Benches

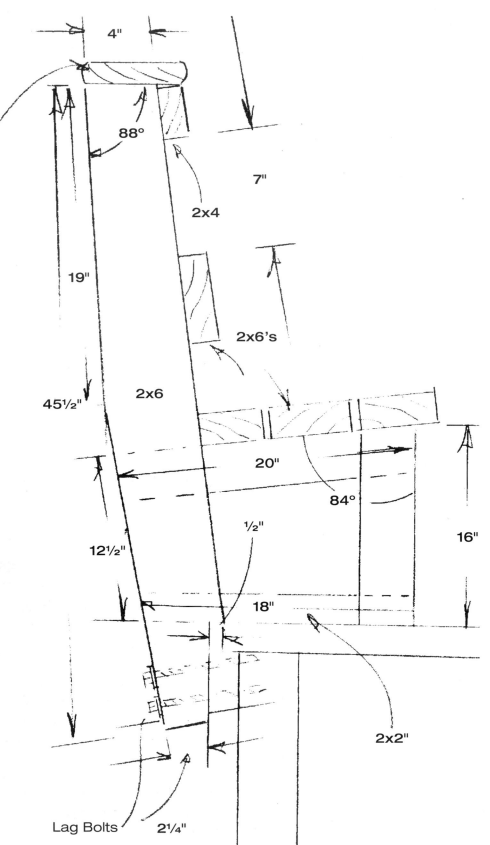

4"

88°

5/4"

19"

7"

2x4

2x6's

45½"

2x6

20"

84°

½"

16"

12½"

18"

2x2"

Lag Bolts   2¼"

Although the railing bench looks complicated, it's fairly easy to build, though it's important to cut the angles correctly (**Drawing**). Cut the back braces first. Lay out a back brace, making sure the angles are correct. Cut one, test-fit it on the deck to make sure it fits correctly; and then use this brace as a pattern to cut as many back braces as you need (**Photo 1**). Assemble the brace and supports for one support frame using 3-inch deck screws (**Photo 2**). Again test-fit it on the deck. Fasten the frame to the deck with ⅜ x 6-inch lag bolts through the back of the back brace, as well as 3-inch deck screws through the bottom support board into the decking boards. Make sure the support frames, especially the back braces, are installed square with the deck and plumb, use a carpenter's square and level to check for both (**Photo 3**).

Deck Rail Benches

Stain or finish the seat boards, rails, and all frames before installation **(Photo 4)**. Fasten the seat boards down on the seat-board supports, again using 3-inch deck screws and making sure the assembly is square and plumb **(Photo 5)**. Attach the 2x4 rails to the back braces with 3-inch deck screws **(Photo 6)**. Fasten the ⁵⁄₄x6 top rail to the tops of the back braces and to the top 2x4 with 2-inch deck screws **(Photo 7)**. Cut end boards to finish off the seats. Round their ends, and fasten them in place with 3-inch deck screws **(Photo 8)**.

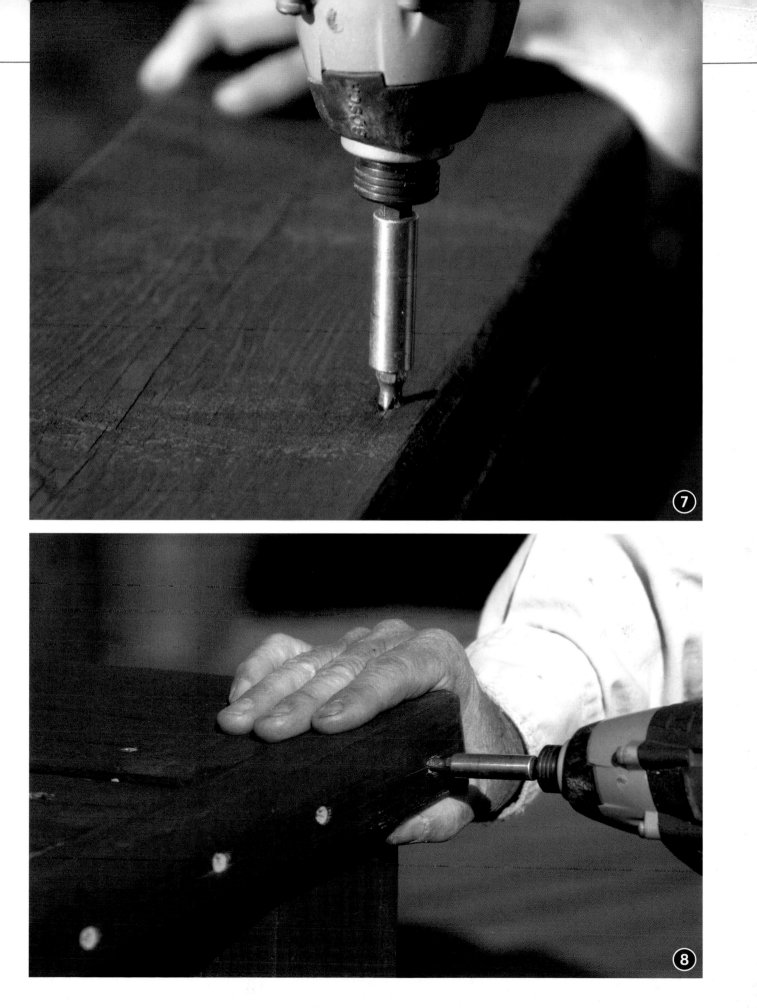

Storage Bench

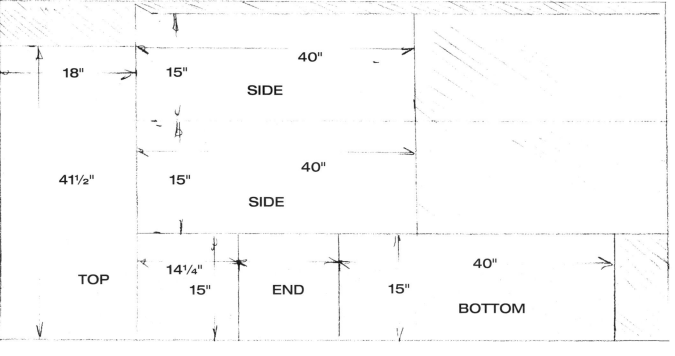

CUTTING PLAN FOR PLYWOOD

18"

15"

40"

SIDE

41½"

15"

40"

SIDE

TOP

14¼"

15"

END

15"

40"

BOTTOM

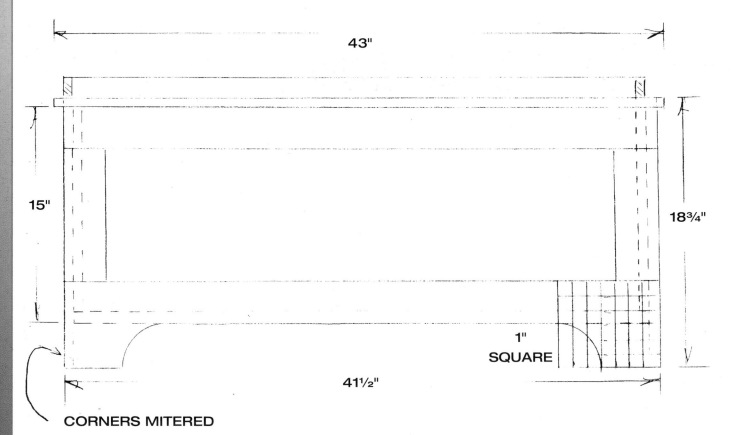

43"

15"

18¾"

1"
SQUARE

41½"

CORNERS MITERED

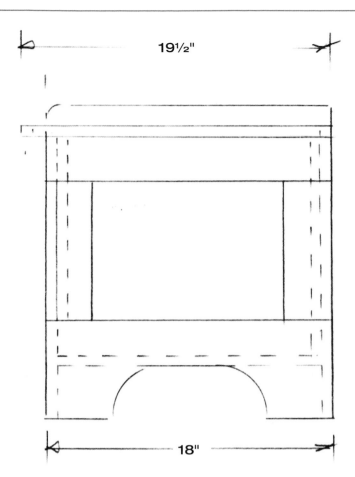

19½"

18"

The first step is to rip the pieces from the ¾-inch 4x8 exterior plywood (**Photo 1**). Lay the plywood on a pair of sawhorses or other support. Using a tape measure, a carpenter's square, and a long straightedge, mark the plywood to be cut following the cutting diagram (**Photo 2**). Using a portable circular saw, cut 24 inches from one end (**Photo 3**).

Rip the remaining piece into three 15-inch pieces. Cut the ends, sides, and bottom from the 15-inch pieces (**Photo 4, page 44**). Fasten the bottom on the bottom end of the end pieces using waterproof glue (**Photo 5, page 44**). Then

Storage Bench

secure the pieces with galvanized nails **(Photo 6)**. One method of holding the end pieces in place while gluing and nailing is with wood clamps **(Photo 7)**.

Fasten the front and back in the same manner **(Photo 8)**, and then paint the bench "box" in the desired color with exterior latex paint. Rip the trim pieces to width using a portable circular saw or table saw **(Photo 9)**. The corners of the trim pieces are mitered. Set a portable circular saw or miter saw at 45-degrees and cut the corners of the trim pieces **(Photo 10)**.

their corners at 45 degrees **(Photo 13)**. Fasten the seat-board trim pieces in place using glue and 6d nails, making sure the mitered corners are neatly fastened together **(Photo 14)**. Fill any cracks between the seat-board trim pieces and the plywood seat board with wood putty. Sand the seat-board smooth, and paint it in the desired color.

Cut the seat-board top pieces to width and length. Round the ends of the side pieces using a saber saw. Paint in the desired color. Fasten the seat board pieces in place with glue and 6d finishing nails driven up through the bottom of the seat board and into the seat-board pieces **(Photo 15)**. Note clamping them in place with wood clamps makes the job easier.

Fasten the seat board in place with a pair of 2-inch hinges attached with screws through the back edge of the seat-board trim and the top back trim piece **(Photo 16)**.

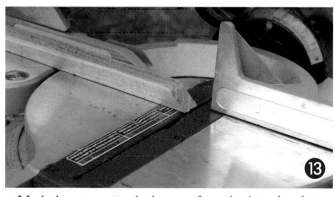

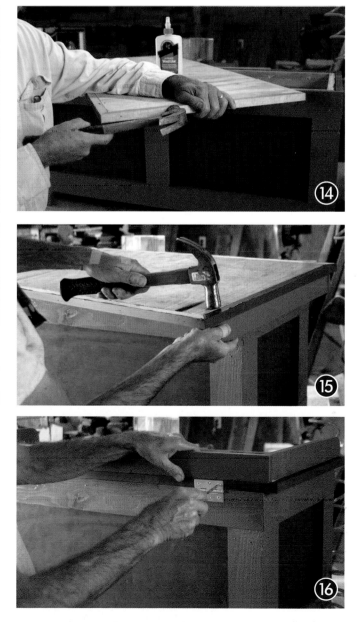

Mark the cutouts in the bottom front, back, and end trim pieces, and cut them out with a saber saw **(Photo 11)**. Then sand the cut edges smooth. Fasten the bottom trim pieces in place with glue and stainless-steel or galvanized 6d nails. Note the corners of the bottom trim protrude below the bench box 3 inches, with the cutout edge flush with the bottom of the bench box. Fasten the top trim pieces with glue and stainless steel or galvanized 6d finish nails. Fasten the corner vertical trim pieces in place in the same manner **(Photo 12)**.

Rip ¾-inch seat-board trim pieces to width, and then cut

Time to Complete: 12-13 Hours

Outdoor Cooking Center

I love to cook outdoors. Not only do I like to grill for family and friends, but I smoke a wide variety of meats, such as brisket, ribs, and chickens, sometimes for a full neighborhood party. My fish fryer also gets a work-out during the summer months. I probably use the turkey fryer the least, only three or four times a year. Over the years I've refined outdoor cooking so it's simple and easy by obtaining the right equipment and creating a comfortable place to cook. A specific area designed for cooking makes it easier not only to cook but to store equipment as well. In many cases outdoor cooking also involves entertaining folks, so you may want to set up your outdoor cooking center so it's suitable to entertaining guests.

OUTDOOR COOKING CENTER

Shopping List:

2 2x4, 10' long

3 2x4, 8' long

Edge form, 12' long

2 Western red cedar, ¾" x 2" , 8' long

2 Western red cedar, ¾" x 1½", 12' long

1 Form board, 1½" x 3½", 12' long

2 Form board, 1½" x 3½", 3' long

1 Form board, ¾" x 5½", 8' long

1 Form board, ¾" x 5½", 3' long

1 Form board, ¾" x 3½", 12' long

1 Form board, ¾" x 3½", 3' long

3 80-lb. bags concrete

1 Bottle concrete color

Cutting List:

4 Side top and bottoms, 1½" x 3½", 5' long

4 Side ends, 1½" x 3½", 27½" long

2 Side center supports, 1½" x 3½", 27½" long

4 End bottom and top supports, 1½" x 3½",
   17" long

1 Top center support, 1½" x 3½", 17" long

6 Support blocks, 1½" x 3½", 6" long

Brown trim

   2 Verticals, ¾" x 2", 31½" long

   2 Horizontals, ¾" x 2", 21½" long

   8 Verticals, ¾" x 2", 32¼" long (door trim)

   8 Horizontals, ¾" x 2", 25¾" long (door trim)

6 Green trim, ¾" x 1½", 31½" long

6 End siding boards, ½" x 5", 19½" long

24 Door siding boards, ½" x 5", 29⅞" long

2 Form board, 1½" x 3½", 64½" long

1 Form board, 1½" x 3½", 29½" long

2 Form board, ¾" x 5½", 64½" long

1 Form board, ¾" x 5½", 29½" long

2 Form board, ¾" x 3½", 64½" long

1 Form board, ¾" x 3½", 29½" long

Outdoor Cooking Center

CHAPTER 2: OUTDOOR COOKING

If you think of them as giant pieces of outdoor "furniture," decks are relatively easy to build. Note: make sure you understand and follow all state and local building codes, rules, and regulations. Decks consist of several components: posts for support; girders or support beams, and decking. Posts may be set in concrete, attached to plates anchored to concrete, or set on precast pier blocks. The method depends on soil conditions and local codes. Ledgers are two-bys anchored to the house wall to support the deck in that location. Headers are two-by anchor points for joists on the outer ends of the deck. Joists are two-by's running from the ledger board to the headers and fastened to both, usually with joist hangers. Decking may be treated wood, western red cedar, California redwood, or composite materials. Wood decking may be 2-by's or ¾-by's.

A giant right triangle—made out of 1x2s, with one 3-foot side, one 4-foot side, and the longest side (the hypotenuse) measuring 5 feet—held with glue and plywood gussets can be used to easily lay out a deck to make sure that it is square.

OUTDOOR COOKING CENTER

Shopping List:

(for Low 12' x 12' deck)

2 Header boards, 2x8, 12' long

1 Ledger board, 2x8, 12' long

8 Joists, 2x8, 14' long

26 Deck boards, ¾x6, 12' long

6 Pier blocks

20 Joist hangers

1 Post, 4x4, 8' long, cut to fit height needed

2" deck screws for deck boards

1" deck screws for joist hangers

3" deck screws for headers and ledger

Cutting List:

(for Low 12' x 12' deck)

Same as shopping list.

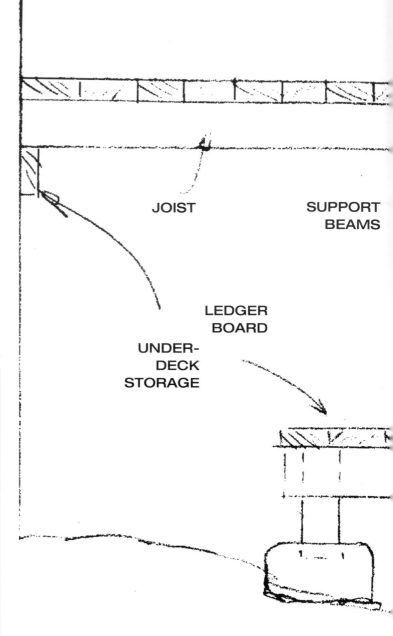

JOIST   SUPPORT BEAMS

LEDGER BOARD

UNDER-DECK STORAGE

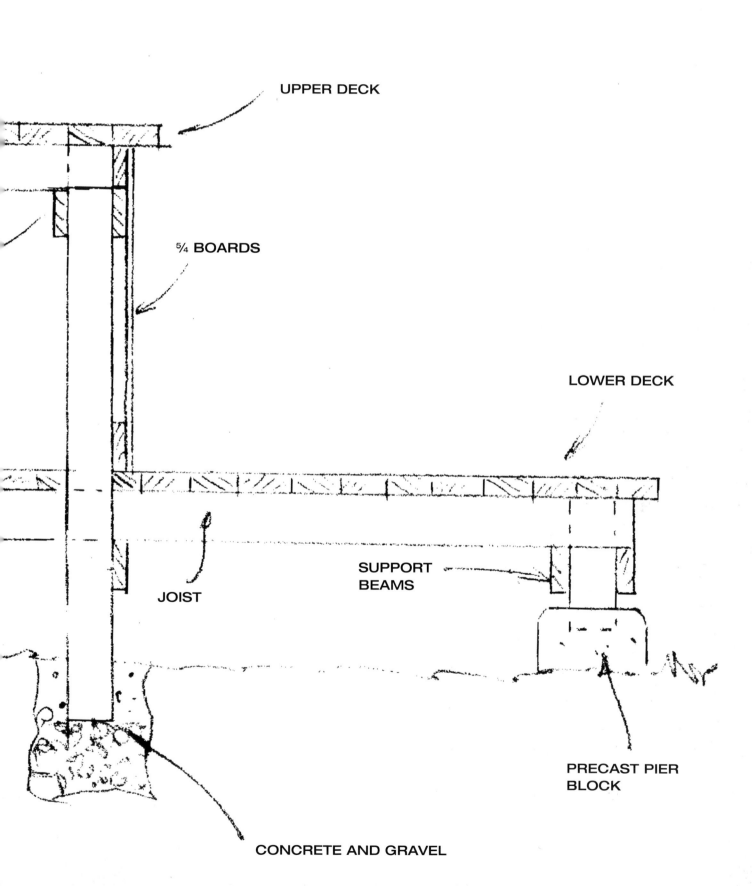

UPPER DECK

⅝ BOARDS

LOWER DECK

JOIST

SUPPORT
BEAMS

PRECAST PIER
BLOCK

CONCRETE AND GRAVEL

Outdoor Cooking Center

The center shown is an add-on, second-level deck below the existing main deck. The lower deck provides an area for a gas grill, a built-in storage area, storage cabinet with a concrete countertop, and space for guests **(Photo 1)**. Gas grills are not quite as messy as charcoal grills, although you may still have some grease problems. (Adjoining the lower deck in my yard is a small brick patio. This provides space for a smoker and fish fryer or in my case fryers for those times when I fry for a big party. No matter how hard you work at it, fish fryers splatter and drop grease, creating a cleanup and safety problem on a deck. By the same token, smokers require filling with hot coals and ashes, a safety problem if done on a wooden deck. And again, grease can be a problem.

The space between the upper and lower decks has doors to create under-deck storage spaces. Depending on your equipment and cooking style, as well as deck or patio space, you may wish to vary the center to suit your needs **(Photos 2, 3, 4)**.

The first step in creating the center shown is to build the lower deck. This is a straightforward, simple deck construction. The deck shown was constructed of residential outdoor re-dried (air-dried after treatment, ADAT) wood. This

makes the wood lighter in weight and ready for immediate finish. A ledger board is fastened to the bottom edge of the upper level deck, making sure it is level. Then lay out the other three sides, using stakes and a string line and string level. The low-level deck shown was supported on precast concrete deck piers, supported on concrete footings. Make sure you follow local codes and regulations on deck support for your area. Use the triangle system of 3, 4, and 5 feet to lay the deck out square. Or you can build a large triangle to check for square. The side headers are then attached to the ends of the ledger board, and the front header fastened between the side headers. Joist hangers provide support for the joists **(Photos 5, 6, 7)**. Non-corrosive fasteners suitable for use with pressure-treated materials were used to assemble the deck. The deck is covered with ¾×6 radius-edge deck boards **(Photos 8, 9)**. The lower deck boards extend beneath the upper deck by 24 inches and are supported on a joist and piers. This provides off-the-ground storage under the deck for items such as fish

Outdoor Cooking Center

fryers, pool covers, and other equipment. You can also add a covering under the deck to protect the gear from rainwater. A number of products are available.

With the deck assembled, the space between the upper and lower deck levels is covered over with ⁵⁄₄x6 deck boards to match the deck **(Photos 10, 11, 12, 13, 14)**. Two large doors are constructed, again using ⁵⁄₄x6 material to provide easy access under the deck. Cleats on the back hold the upright boards together **(Photo 15)**. A cross-brace prevents the doors from eventually sagging. Large hinges and a sliding lock keep the doors in place **(Photo 16)**. The deck, as well as

(14)

(15)

(16)

age. The first step in constructing the storage counter is to frame the sides with 2x4s, fastening with 3-inch deck screws **(Photo 18)**. Fasten a center vertical divider/support 2x4 in place flush with the outside edges of the top and bottom 2x4s **(Drawing B, page 54)**. The outside frame on the project shown is positioned 4 inches in from the edge of the deck. Put the frame in place, and use a square to make sure it is squared with the facers between the upper and lower decks and is properly spaced from the deck edge. Level the top, providing a slight rise at the upper deck side for drainage. Use wood shims to achieve the level desired. Fasten

(17)

(18)

the vertical ¾x6 facers and doors are all finished with one-coat wood finish in Cedar tone. A large brush or roller makes it easy to apply the material to the deck **(Photo 17)**.

The storage cabinet is situated at the end of the deck (and next to the brick patio in my yard). Doors on both sides allow access for equipment for the gas grill on the deck side and for charcoal and frying oil on the other side for the smoker and fryers. The side facing the deck and gas grill has a shelf.

All frame work for the storage cabinet is pressure-treated 2x4 lumber. It is not exposed to food prep or food stor-

(19)

Outdoor Cooking Center

the bottom plate down to the deck and into the joists. With the bottom anchored, use a level to plumb the frame, and secure the upper-deck-side end to the upper deck or vertical facer boards. Assemble the inside frame in the same manner. Locate the inside frame the proper distance from the outer frame, and anchor the bottom plate. Make sure the frame is square, and anchor the upper-deck-side end of the frame to the vertical facers. Fasten a 2x4 support block between the frames at the upper-deck end, anchoring it to the vertical facers. Do the same for the bottom, between the frames.

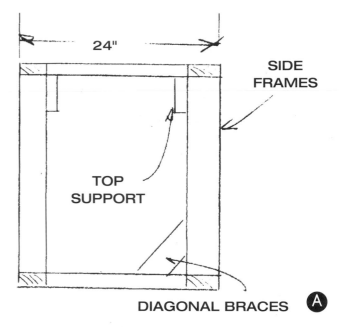

END VIEW

24"

SIDE FRAMES

TOP SUPPORT

DIAGONAL BRACES (A)

(20)

Cut a top spacer for the outer end. This spacer is supported by blocks fastened to the inside edges of the side frames. Position the spacer in place; make sure the opposite frame is plumb; and fasten it in place **(Photo 19)**. Cut a bottom spacer for the outer end, and anchor it to the deck; then anchor the bottom of the frames to it. Cut a diagonal brace; plumb up one side; and fasten the brace in place **(Photo 20)**. Then anchor the opposite diagonal brace in place. A center top spacer is added, supporting it on 2x4 blocks anchored to the center vertical supports.

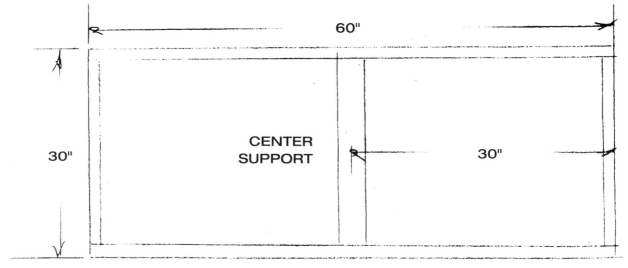

60"

30"

CENTER SUPPORT

30"

(B)

into the 1x6 form boards **(Photo 22)**. The edge form easily wraps around corners without mitering, but you will need a clamp to pull it in place to fasten. The countertop shown utilized slightly rounded corners on the outside. A ½-inch plywood sheathing deck is then placed down on the top support boards, leaving space for the overhang. The plywood edges should be cut at a 45-degree angle to provide more edge support **(Drawing C)**. The plywood is anchored to the supports with screws.

The next step is to pour the concrete countertop. The countertop shown is poured in place, and the first step is to create the form **(Photo 21)**. The edges of the countertop are formed using a split-face granite edge form to create a unique natural-looking stone type texture. Made of high-quality polyurethane, the forms are easy to install. The first step is to add a 2x4 support form around the cabinet. These are held in place with screws to the framework. In the case of the top shown, an additional 2x4 spacer was used to allow for the extra width of the cabinet doors and sides. A 1x6 form is then added to the 2x4 forms. Then the countertop edge forms are installed in place. It's important that the edge form extend slightly above the 1x6 form boards. The edge form is held in place with finishing nails driven from the inside and

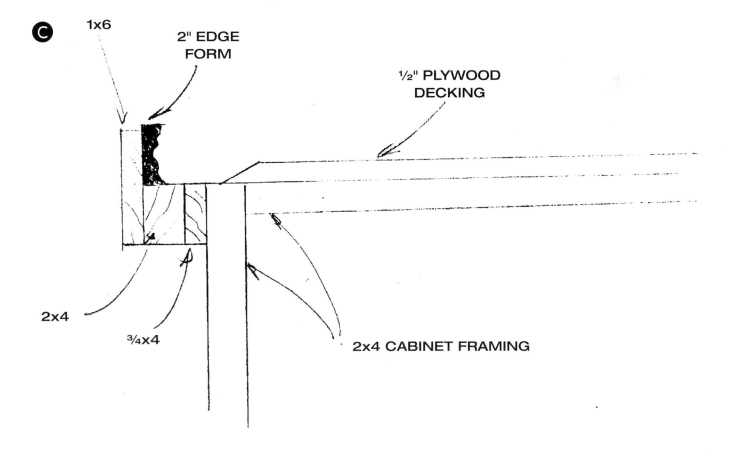

You then mix the concrete. The best choice is to buy a bagged mixture. The countertop shown required three 80-pound bags. One bottle of liquid cement color in terra-cotta was added to the mix **(Photo 23)**. The cement coloring agent is added to water and thoroughly mixed, then added to the dry concrete mix **(Photo 24)**. Add only enough water at a time to blend the mix and water. For the mix shown you can start with ½ gallon of water per bag. A power mixer makes the chore easier, but I made the mix shown in a large wheelbarrow using a concrete hoe to mix the ingredients thoroughly **(Photo 25)**. Once thoroughly mixed, with the coloring evenly distributed, shovel or use a small plastic bucket to pour the concrete into the form, using a trowel to spread it around as needed. You may wish to place drop clothes around the cabinet to prevent getting material onto the wooden deck. Once the form is filled, tap all around the sides with a hammer to settle the concrete and remove any air bubbles **(Photo 26)**. Use a smooth board as a screed to drag off excess concrete, moving the board in a see-sawing motion as you pull off the concrete **(Photo 27)**. Use a trowel to fill in any low spots as you screed and

Outdoor Cooking Center

then use a wooden float to remove excess water and further smooth the surface. Allow the concrete to set until it just slightly dents; then use a smooth-faced metal trowel to work the surface **(Photo 28)**. The more you trowel and the more pressure you apply, the finer the surface finish will be. Allow the concrete to cure. For a moist cure, and stronger pour, lightly mist the surface after troweling and cover with plastic sheeting. The countertop should be protected with a concrete sealer to provide protection from water damage, freeze/thaw cycles, and chipping. Concrete sealer can be applied while the surface is still damp but not wet. Or you can apply water sealer 30 days after the pour. After 24 hours of curing, remove the form boards. Curing should be continued for five days in warm weather and up to seven days in cold weather. Do not allow the concrete to freeze until completely cured.

The top shown was left as is, but doing so risks staining. You can grind and polish the top to a high sheen and use a gloss sealer if you prefer. To grind and polish, use an angle grinder or orbital sander with progressively finer grits, using water as a slurry on the top. Note: Make sure you use a GFCI-protected circuit for this chore.

The next step is to finish the cabinet by adding the covering and doors. The cabinet shown was covered with western red cedar lap siding and rough-sawn board trim to match the siding and trim on the house. The siding pieces were first treated with waterproof sealant, and the trim strips with waterproof sealant plus tinted wood protector.

The cedar siding for the fixed portions, including the end, are first fastened in place using stainless-steel siding nails **(Photo 29)**. The brown-stained wooden trim strips are added over the siding using stainless steel finishing nails. Then the green-painted accent strips are fastened in place with stainless-steel finishing nails **(Photo 30)**. Wooden facer trim boards are added to the areas surrounding the doors. The doors are constructed using siding and brown-stained trim boards. They are assembled by placing the cut trim siding boards in place on a smooth, flat surface, then attaching the siding boards to their backs with wood glue and staples driven from the siding into the trim boards **(Photo 31)**. The doors are hung with hidden hinges and held in place with heavy-duty magnetic catches. Green-painted knobs finish off the cabinet. Add chairs and table for entertaining guests while you cook.

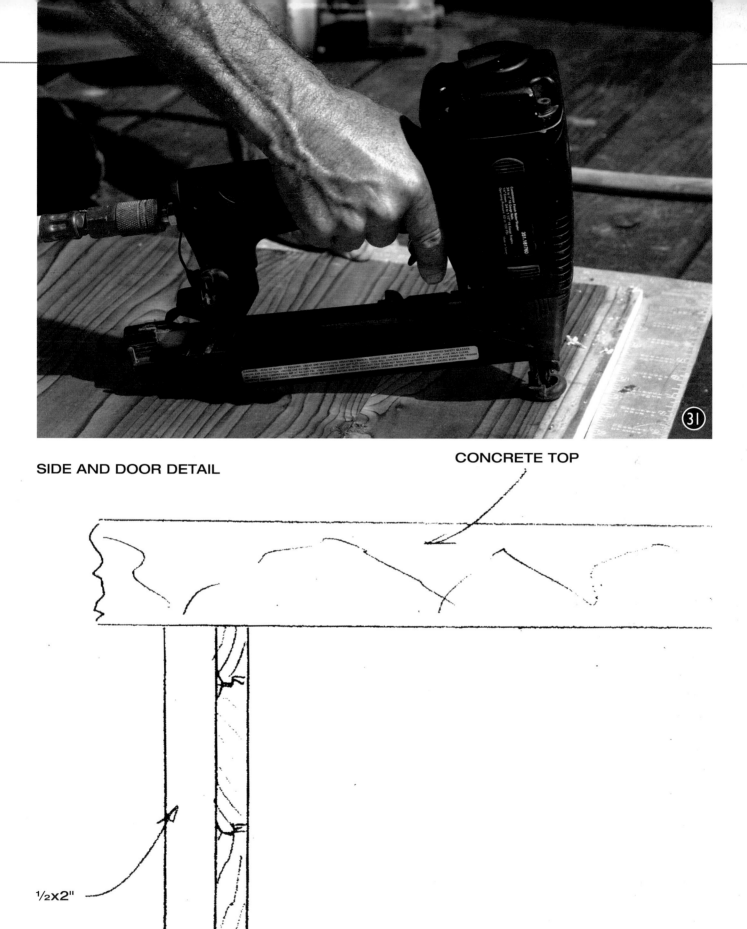

SIDE AND DOOR DETAIL

CONCRETE TOP

½x2"

WESTERN RED CEDAR TRIM

D

BBQ Station

Aplace to hold BBQ tools and charcoal—and a big flat surface for holding that platter of steaks about to go onto the grill—can make outdoor grilling easier and more fun. The BBQ station shown is that and more. Featuring casters, it can be rolled out of the way on your deck, then moved to the grill when you need it. The height is a bit unusual as well, so the roll-around cart can also be used as a stand-up bar. We all know friends like to converse and enjoy each others' (and your) company while you do your BBQ chores, and this provides space for several to sip cool drinks while you do the work alongside. The station shown was made of pressure-treated ⁵⁄₄-by decking, but a good choice would be redwood or western red cedar. If the cart is to be stored in a garage or shed when not in use, even pine could be used. The casters allowing the cart to roll should also be lockable. You don't want it (and your guests) rolling across the deck while in use. Lockable casters allow for easy mobility for storage after the party.

Time to Complete: 3-4 Hours

BBQ STATION

Shopping List:
8 Pressure-treated ⁵⁄₄x6, 8' long
2" locking casters
2" deck screws
3 Screw hooks, or as needed

Cutting List:
8 Leg pieces, ⁵⁄₄" x 2½" x 36"
4 Front and back horizontals,
    ⁵⁄₄" x 2½" x 36"
4 Side horizontals, ⁵⁄₄" x 2½" x 24"
5 Top pieces, ⁵⁄₄" x 5½" x 48"
4 Shelf pieces, ⁵⁄₄" x 5½" x 26"

BBQ Station

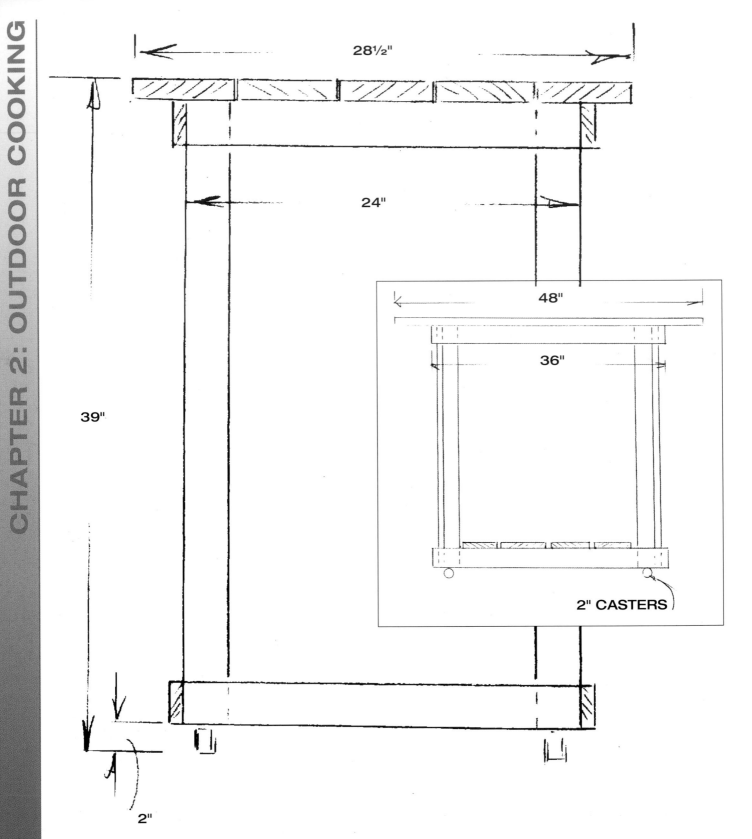

28½"

24"

39"

48"

36"

2" CASTERS

2"

The bottom shelf provides storage space for charcoal and other large items **(Photo 4)**.

Install push-in casters in holes drilled into the bottom ends of the L-shape legs **(Photo 5)**.

Add the screw-hooks for holding BBQ tools, and coat the station in the finish of your choice **(Photo 6)**.

Although the height shown provides a lot of versatility, you can make the cart lower or higher to suit **(Drawings)**. As the legs are made of fairly thin material, they are created by fastening two pieces into an L-shape. First step is to rip the ¾ material to 2½ inches wide. This can easily be done with a portable circular saw and a rip-gauge **(Photo 1)**, or on a table saw.

Fasten the narrow leg pieces together to create the L-supports, using 2-inch deck screws in predrilled holes **(Photo 2)**.

Assemble the station using deck screws in predrilled holes **(Photo 3)**.

Time to Complete: 4-5 Hours

Classic Redwood Picnic Table and Benches

This classic redwood picnic table and its benches, made of construction common grade wood, are a modification of the popular Sonoma picnic table from the California Redwood Association. The beauty of redwood, combined with its natural resistance to insects and its durability, has made this a traditional classic material for picnic tables and other outdoor projects. All fasteners must be of noncorrosive materials such as aluminum, stainless steel, or top-quality hot-dipped galvanized screws or nails. Ordinary nails and screws will cause stains.

You need to decide whether or not to apply a finish. Left as is, or unfinished, the redwood will provide a beautiful table and benches but will eventually turn into a soft driftwood gray color. Redwood will accept a number of finishes. Some will bring out the natural beauty of redwood; others can be used to harmonize or contrast with surrounding structures. A clear, water repellent finish is the simplest and is recommended to stabilize the color at its natural reddish tan. Semitransparent stains in "redwood" shades can also be used to tint the wood without hiding the grain. If you choose to hide the grain and use solid-color paints or stains, apply them over an oil-based primer.

CLASSIC REDWOOD PICNIC TABLE AND BENCHES	Cutting List:
Shopping List for table and two benches:	**Table**
5 2x6, 10' long	5 Top boards, 1½" x 5½" x 60"
4 2x4, 8' long	2 Cleats, 1½" x 3½" x 27"
2 2x4, 10' long	4 Legs, 1½" x 3½" x 40"
Hardware: 12 sets machine bolts, washers, and nuts, ¼" x 3½";	2 Braces, 1½" x 3½" x 23½"
6 sets ¼" x 3½" lag screws with washers; 4" deck screws	**Benches**
	4 Top boards, 1½" x 5½" x 60"
	4 Cleats, 1½" x 3½" x 10½"
	8 Legs, 1½" x 3½" x 19½"
	4 Braces, 1½" x 3½" x 15"

Classic Redwood Picnic Table and Benches

Position a cleat in place, allowing ½-inch between the cleat ends and the edges of the tabletop. Fasten the cleat to the top boards with 4-inch deck screws driven down through the countersunk holes. Make sure the screws don't penetrate through the top pieces **(Photo 3)**.

Cut the legs to length. They should be 40 inches in length with a 38-degree angle on top and bottom. Fasten one leg to the cleat with a C-clamp, making sure the angled end fits snugly down onto the tabletop board. Then position the opposite leg in position down on the tabletop board and against the first leg. C-clamp the two legs together at the position they cross. Adjust the legs slightly to create a cross with a 28½-inch outside measurement from the tabletop bottom to the bottom corner of the leg. Then mark the cuts for the cross-lap joints of the legs on each leg **(Photo 4)**.

To cut the cross-lap joints, first mark the angles, width, and depth of the cuts. Then use a handsaw to make several cuts down to the depth lines on both sides of the stock. It's important for the depth and angles to be correct **(Photo 5)**.

Use a chisel to remove the partially sawn wood strips from the cross-lap joint and smooth up the joint **(Photo 6)**. Once you have cut the cross laps, clamp the legs back together again. Locate the position for the bolts in the leg ends, as well as for the lag screw in the center of the cross-lap joint. Counterbore these locations with a forstner bit in a portable electric drill **(Photo 7)**.

Position one leg set in place, and anchor it to the cleat

Classic Redwood Picnic Table and Benches

⑧

using machine bolts **(Photo 8)**. Then cut a brace to length with 45-degree angles on each end. Place the brace in position. Use a carpenter's square to make sure the leg set is square with the bottom of the table. Then fasten the brace top to the underside of the table with countersunk wood screws **(Photo 9)**. Fasten the lower end to the leg joint using a lag screw through the cross lap of the leg assembly and into the lower end of the brace **(Photo 10)**.

Note: You should countersink all the bolt holes to accommodate the bolt heads and washers. Once all bolts have been installed, remove the C-clamps and bar clamps. Repeat this step for the opposite leg.

Note: If you start with the same leg, for instance the left-hand side, on the opposite end of the table, you will find that

WOODWORKER'S TIP

It's often more efficient to cut all of your components for a project before starting any actual construction. This will make it easier if you cut your parts in a garage or basement shop and then construct your project outdoors—you'll make fewer trips. Plus, if you are short of materials, you'll discover early and won't have to run to the home center in the middle of the project.

you won't have to change the angles of the dadoes.

The benches are constructed in the same basic manner **(Photo 11)** except the angles on the legs are different.

Round the corners of the bench tops in the same man-ner as for the tabletop **(Photo 12)**, and then sand all edges smooth. Sand the table and bench tops to make sure there are no splinters sticking up from installing the fasteners **(Photo 13)**.

Serving Cart

Time to Complete: 4-5 Hours

Regardless of whether your outdoor cooking is on a deck or patio or under a sunroof, a serving cart can be a great entertaining helpmate. The cart shown features a tiled top. Not only is the tile easy to clean, but it also holds hot food plates. The tile top adds to the decor of the cart as well. The cart is made of California redwood, not only because of the beauty of the wood, but because it's easy to work and long lasting. Although the cart shown was left unfinished, you may wish to stain or paint it to match your deck or patio. The redwood lumber can be purchased in widths needed, so no ripping of materials is required. The cart is fairly easy to construct, although it looks like a "bragging piece."

SERVING CART

Shopping List:
2 2x4, 8' long
3 1x4, 10' long
1 ¾" exterior plywood, 4' x 4' long
1 1" Dowel, 22" long
2 6" Wheels
4 Washers
1 1½" Threaded rod, 36" long
2 ½" Locknuts
30 4"x4" ceramic tile
Waterproof tile adhesive
Waterproof tile grout

Cutting List:
2 Legs, 1½" x 3½" x 35½"
2 Legs, 1½" x 3½" x 34½"
1 Top, ¾" x 22" x 26"
2 Top front & back boards, ¾" x 3½" x 22"
2 Top side boards, ¾" x 3½" x 32½"
2 Shelf support boards, ¾" x 3½" x 22"
2 Shelf supports, ¾" x 3½" x 26¾"
5 Shelf boards, ¾" x 3½" x 23½"

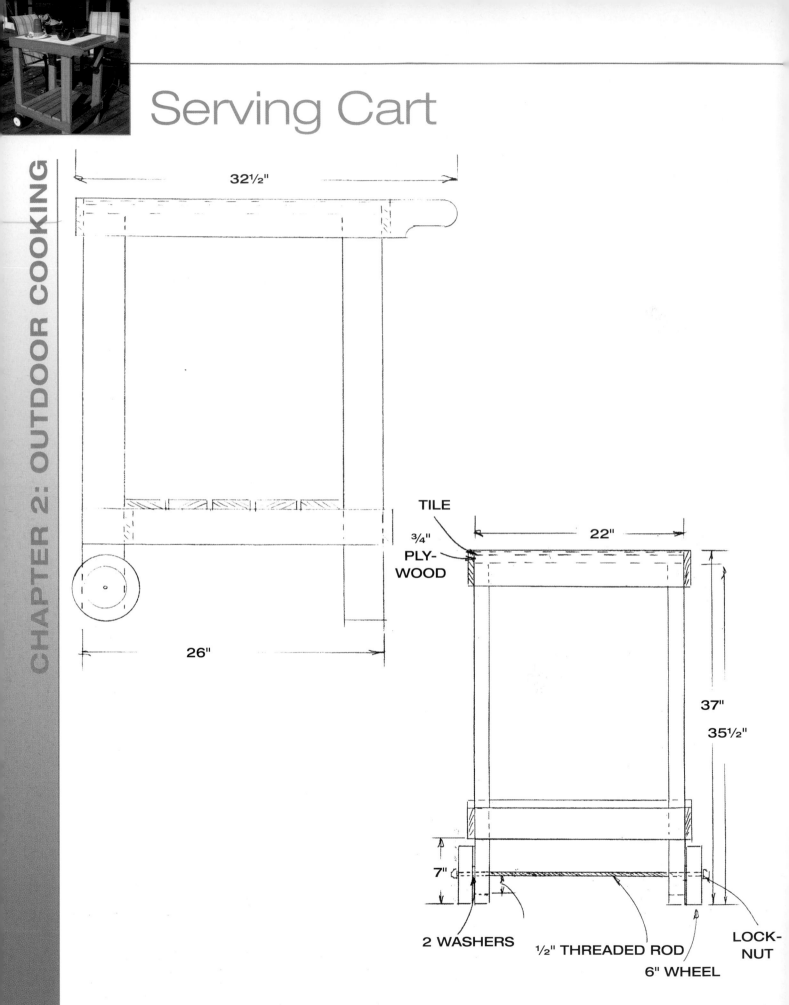

Serving Cart

32½"

26"

TILE

¾"

PLY-
WOOD

22"

37"

35½"

7"

2 WASHERS

½" THREADED ROD

LOCK-
NUT

6" WHEEL

The first step is to cut a piece of exterior plywood to the correct size following the drawings. Apply a waterproof tile adhesive to the plywood, and position the tiles in place. Note the tile should be spaced ⅛ inch from the edge of the board to allow grout to fill in between tile and front, back, and side pieces **(Photo 1)**. Cut the front and back top pieces to the correct length, and fasten them in place with waterproof glue and stainless-steel finishing nails **(Photo 2)**.

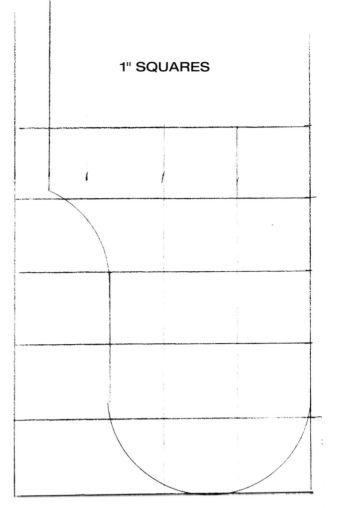

Enlarge the square drawing, and create the pattern for the handle ends on the side pieces; then cut them out using a saber saw. Fasten the side pieces to the top board, again with glue and nails. Set all nails slightly below the wood surface with a nail set. Turn the assembled top upside down on a work surface; cut the legs to length; then measure and locate the threaded steel rod "axle" holes in the two short legs. Bore using a ½-inch bit **(Photo 3)**.

Fasten the legs in place inside the corners of the top edges using waterproof glue and 1½-inch stainless-steel screws, or deck screws. Predrill the holes with a ⅛-inch bit to prevent splitting out the soft wood **(Photo 4)**. Turn the

1" SQUARES

Serving Cart

cart over so the axle side is down. Thread a pair of washers and a wheel on the threaded steel axle rod, and then turn a locknut on one end. Push the threaded rod through the holes in both of the short legs **(Photo 5)**.

Cut a horizontal support piece, and fasten it in place with glue and stainless-steel nails, making sure it is square **(Photo 6)**. Add another pair of washers and the second wheel, and turn on the locknut to secure both wheels in place **(Photo 7)**. Saw off the excess threaded rod using a hacksaw, and smooth up the cut end with a file.

Stand the cart upright; cut the bottom shelf support boards to length; and install them with glue and screws. Cut the shelf boards, and fasten them in place with waterproof glue and stainless-steel nails **(Photo 8)**.

Cut the handle to length, and install it between the sides with the waterproof glue and a single stainless-steel screw into each end **(Photo 9)**. Tape the edges of the top pieces with masking tape, and apply grout to the tile, following the grout manufacturer's instructions. Clean off all grout before it sets **(Photo 10)**.

Time to Complete: 4-5 Hours

Children's Picnic Table

A picnic table just for the kids can be a great family backyard addition. This pint-sized table is fun for all and is an easy project. It's made entirely of California heart-grade redwood. Not only does this long-lasting table take weathering and abuse, but the soft wood is easily worked, and the beauty of the wood provides a great addition to backyard decor. You can leave the table as is—without a finish—and it will weather to a beautiful gray color, and that's the safest. Or you can use an oil deck finish. Make sure any finish is labeled for use with food.

CHILDREN'S PICNIC TABLE

Shopping List:

3 2x4, 8' long

4 2x6, 8' long

3" deck screws

Cutting List:

4 Legs, 1½" x 3½" x 21"

2 Top end braces, 1½" x 3½" x 22" (cut to fit)

2 Bottom end braces, 1½" x 3½" x 40" (cut to fit)

2 Seat boards, 1½" x 5½" x 48"

5 Top boards, 1½" x 5½" x 48"

2 Center braces, 1½" x 3½" x 19" (cut to fit)

Children's Picnic Table

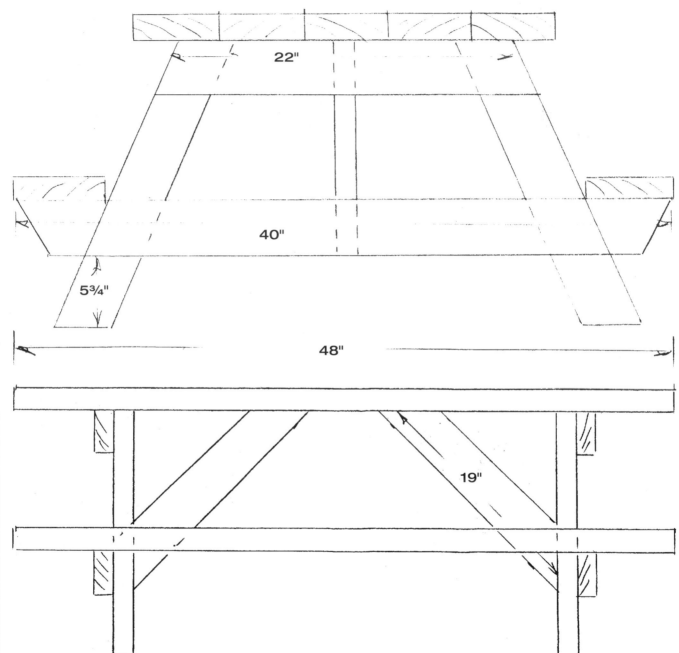

22"

40"

5¾"

48"

19"

Although the table looks complicated, it's simple to build, but it does have several angles to cut **(Drawings)**. First step is to cut the legs at the proper lengths and angles. Cut the top and bottom ends of the legs at 65 degrees. You can use a protractor to determine the angles on one leg and mark with a straight edge or side of a square. If you have a miter saw, set the saw at 25 degrees. This will create the proper angle **(Photo 1)**. Cut one leg, and then cut the other three legs using the first leg as the pattern. Even if the angle isn't

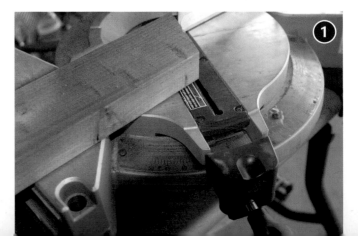

exactly 65 degrees, the legs will all match and create a table that will sit level.

Cut the top and bottom end braces to the proper angles in the same fashion. Then lay a pair of legs on a smooth, flat surface. Position the top end piece across the legs, and drive one 3-inch deck screw in place on each end of the assembly **(Photo 2)**.

Measure up 5¾ inches from the bottom of each leg, and make a mark. Then make a mark 4½ inches back from the ends on the top side of the bottom brace. Position the bottom brace in place; check the top brace to make sure all cut edges are even; then drive a screw down through the bottom brace into each leg **(Photo 3)**. Again check to make sure the assembly aligns properly, and then drive a second screw into

each joint. Repeat for the opposite end frame.

To assemble the table, position each end frame on a smooth, flat surface such as a garage or shop floor. Use a wood clamp on the bottom ends to help hold the end frames upright. Or you might get help from one of your little friends for this chore. Measure from each end of the top end-frame brace to determine the center. Make a mark on each end-frame top piece. Then measure from that mark 2¾ inches toward the outside edge of the end frame, and make another mark on each end frame. This determines the location of the center top board. Cut a top board to length. Measure 6 inches from both ends, and make a mark. With these marks, position the top board in place and fasten with two 3-inch deck screws on both ends **(Photo 4)**. Set the

Sandbox

Time to Complete: 2-3 Hours

A sandbox is one of the most appreciated children's projects. With only a handful of toys, children will play in a sandbox for hours. Yet, the sandbox shown is also one of the simplest of outdoor furniture projects. With only a few tools you can build a "heritage" project enjoyed by lots of kids. Because it will be in contact with the ground and must hold moist sand, a sandbox should be made of a soft, yet sturdy, water and insect-resistant wood. Redwood is a top choice for this project. Redwood is soft, machines easily, and doesn't splinter,

another must for children's outdoor furniture projects. Because the box must be sturdy, it is fastened together with 3-inch deck screws. The box does not have a bottom, so you may wish to place a grass barrier of black plastic down before adding the sand.

SANDBOX

Shopping List:

4 Redwood 2x6, 10' long

2 Redwood 2x4, 10' long

2 Redwood 2x4, 8' long

52 3" deck screws

Cutting List:

8 Side pieces, 1½" x 5½" x 5'

4 Upright braces, 1½" x 3½" x 11½"

4 Corner blocks, small, 1½" x 3½" x 7"
 (cut to fit)

4 Corner blocks, large, 1½" x 3½" x 14"
 (cut to fit)

4 Top side edges, 1½" x 3½" x 5"
 (cut to fit)

Time to Complete: 1-3 Hours Each

DECK RAIL PLANTER BOX

Planter Boxes

Flower planter boxes are fun to build and fun to use. We show three different planters. Two of the planters were made from scraps left from building a deck. One planter was made from scraps left from siding the house with western red cedar siding and lumber.

LARGE PLANTER BOX

DECK RAIL PLANTER BOX
Shopping List:
1 Pressure-treated deck board, 5/4x6, 8' long

6d Galvanized finishing nails

Cutting List:
1 Bottom, 1" x 5½" x 22"

2 Ends, 1" x 5½" x 6"

2 Sides, 1" x 5½" x 24"

LARGE PLANTER BOX
Shopping List:
1 Pressure-treated deck board, 5/4x6, 14' long

2 Pressure-treated deck boards, 5/4x6, 8' long

1 Pressure-treated 2x4, 8' long

4d Galvanized nails

Screws or 8d galvanized nails

Cutting List:
12 Side pieces, 1" x 5½" x 13"

4 Side top and bottom cleats, 1½" x 3½" x 16½"

4 Side top and bottom cleats, 1½" x 3½" x 14½"

3 Bottom pieces, 1" x 5½" x 16¼"

4 Posts, 1½" x 1½" x 16"

SIDING PLANTER BOX
Shopping List:
1 Cedar siding, 5" wide by 8' long

1 Treated 2x4, 8' long

1 Rough-sawn cedar, 1x12, 10' long

4d Galvanized nails

Cutting List:
8 Side pieces, ½" x 5" x 12"

4 Legs, 1½" x 1½" x 11"

8 Corner trim pieces, ¾" x 1½" x 10"

4 Decorative corner trim pieces, ¾" x ¾" x 10"

4 Cleats, ¾" x ¾" x 9"

Top, ¾" x 15" x 15" (cut from three pieces of stock)

4 Top trim, ¾" x 1½" x 16½"

SIDING PLANTER BOX

Deck-Rail Planter Box

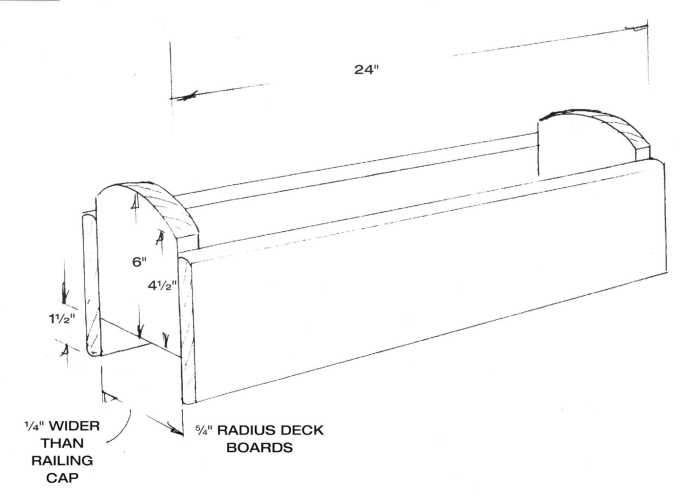

24"

6"

4½"

1½"

¼" WIDER THAN RAILING CAP

⁵⁄₄" RADIUS DECK BOARDS

① 1

This little planter box is designed to sit over a deck railing. It can also be placed on a deck or patio, on a step, or on a sidewalk for adding instant color. The small planter is also extremely simple to build and requires little in the way of materials. In fact, you may wish to build several while you're at it. Pressure-treated ⁵⁄₄-by decking boards are used to create the planter. You could also make it from stock pine or 1×6 redwood.

If the planter is to sit on a deck railing, the first step is to measure the railing width. The inside bottom of the planter should be ¼ inch wider than the railing **(drawing)**.

If you're using ⁵⁄₄-by lumber, you should rip the radius edges off to create flat edges for the bottom and ends. In some instances you will also have to rip a narrower piece and glue and tack-nail the two together to create the width needed, for both the bottom and ends **(Photo 1)**. Or you can simply rip a pine 1×8 to the width needed.

CHAPTER 4: FOR GARDNERS

Cut the bottom and end pieces to their correct lengths **(Photo 2)**.

Then cut the rounded tops of the end pieces. To simplify this chore, I find a bucket, can, or jar that is of a close radius and mark around it for the corners. Or you can use a compass to mark the radius. Cut the radius on the ends using a saber saw, and then sand it smooth with a piece of sandpaper **(Photo 3)**.

Fasten the ends to the bottom edges using 6d galvanized finishing nails **(Photo 4)**. Predrill the end pieces with a ¹⁄₁₆ -inch bit to prevent splitting .

Fasten the sides to the ends and bottom, again predrilling and using 6d galvanized nails **(Photo 5)**. Sand smooth, and apply a finish of your choice.

Note: the planter can be left as is to weather to a nice gray, stained or finished with a deck stain/oil, or even painted to match house and deck trim.

Large Planter Box

16"

13"

16½"

CLEATS

This planter is also made of pressure-treated materials to complement a wooden deck and matching rail seats. Redwood would also be a good wood choice, and would provide a "softer" look. This planter is big enough to hold a mixture of flowers, and it can double as a patio planter for tomato or pepper plants. In this case, add a wooden trellis to the back to support the plants. This planter is also fairly easy to construct **(drawing)**.

First step is to cut all side pieces to their correct lengths **(Photo 1)**.

Rip stock to create the width needed for the top and bottom cleats. Then cut the top and bottom cleats for two sides to length **(Photo 2)**.

Fasten the cleats to the inside edges of the top and bottom of the pieces for one side **(Photo 3)**. Use 2-inch deck screws for ⁵⁄₄-by material, 1¼-inch deck screws for one-by material. Predrill the cleats with a ¹⁄₁₆-inch bit to prevent splitting. You can also fasten the cleats to the side pieces with 4d galvanized nails.

Cut the cleats for the two remaining sides, and fasten them to the side pieces in the same manner. Note: these

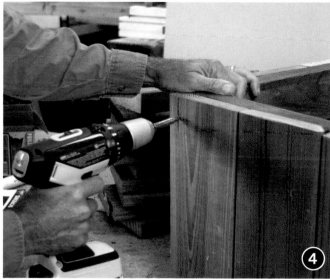

cleats are cut shorter. Fasten the three sides together using screws or 8d galvanized nails in predrilled holes; then fasten the fourth side in place in the same manner. Make sure the assembly sits square **(Photo 4)**.

Cut pieces for the bottom to length, and fasten them in place with screws down through them into the bottom cleats **(Photo 5)**.

Rip the corner support posts from a 2×4, and fasten the corner posts to the edges of the sides with deck screws **(Photo 6)**.

The planter can be left as is or finished. In this case a protective coating of finish was applied to match the planter to the deck and railing seats.

Time to Complete: 3-4 Hours

Planting Arbor

An old-fashioned rose arbor or arbor to hold climbing vines such as wisteria, clematis, or others can add to the enjoyment as well as the decor of your backyard. An arbor is also fairly easy to make. The arbor shown, made of California redwood, is anchored in place to concrete poured into holes. You can set the uprights in concrete first, and then assemble the arbor, but it's easier to assemble the arbor and then have someone help you set the ends into the holes. Another choice is to build the arbor, pour the concrete in the holes, and then anchor the arbor to the concrete using angle irons and concrete anchor screws. In this case, the bottom will need a temporary brace until the arbor is anchored in place. This arbor shown will weather to a beautiful gray color. As an alternative, pressure-treated wood could be used to match a deck or other backyard projects.

PLANTING ARBOR

Shopping List:

4 2x4, 10' long

3 2x4, 8' long

Cutting List:

4 Uprights, 1½" x 3½" x 72"

2 Top cross pieces, 1½" x 3½" x 48"

12 Side pieces, 1½" x 1½" x 24"

4 Rafters, 1½" x 3½" x 30" (cut to fit)

4 Corner braces, 1½" x 3½" x 12" (cut to fit)

6 Top cross pieces, 1½" x 1½" x 27"

Planting Arbor

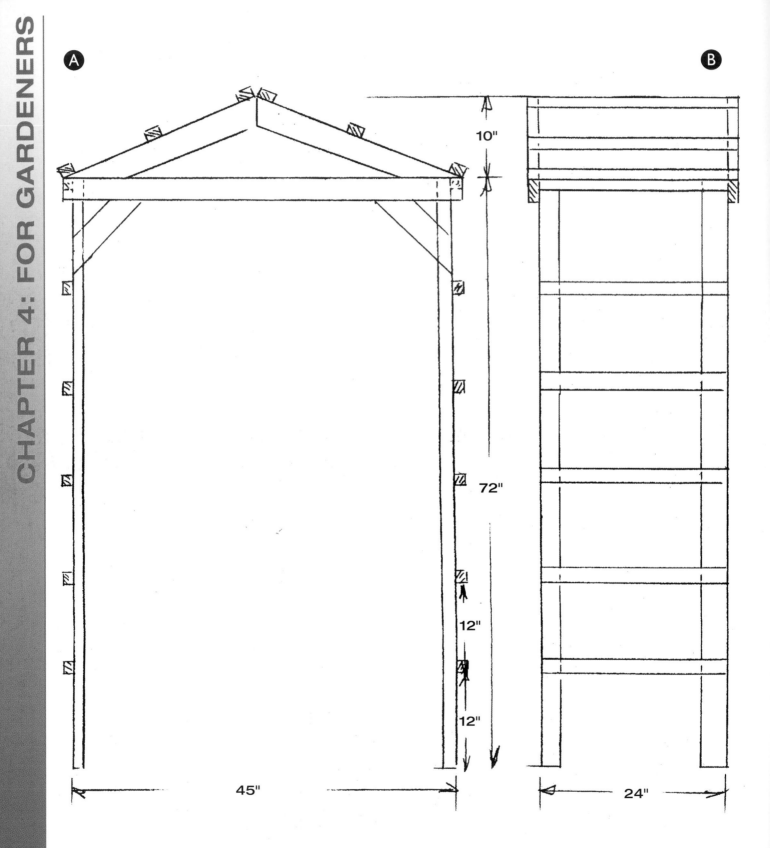

A

B

10"

72"

12"

12"

45"

24"

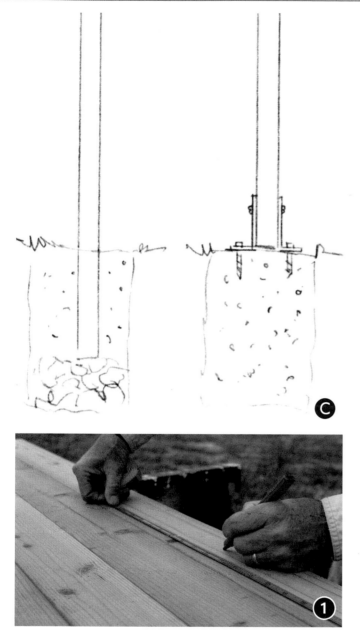

This project is fairly small, so I chose 2x4 uprights as the support structure. You can also enlarge the arbor if you choose, but you would need to use 4x4 poles in that case **(Drawings A and B)**. You can select a variety of methods to support and anchor the arbor **(Drawing C)**. The first step is to cut all four of the 2x4 uprights to length. Lay them on a flat surface, and measure for the side pieces **(Photo 1)**. Using a square, mark the locations for the side pieces on all four uprights **(Photo 2)**.

Rip the side pieces to 1½ x 1½ inches; then anchor them in place with galvanized or stainless-steel nails, making sure the assembly is square **(Photo 3)**. Stand the assembled sides on one side on a smooth, flat surface. Cut the top front and rear cross-pieces, and anchor them to the side assemblies. Make sure the assembly is square **(Photo 4)**.

Planting Arbor

⑤

⑥

Predrill all holes, and use 3-inch deck screws or stainless screws to assemble **(Photo 5)**. Lay out the front and rear "rafters." The easiest method of doing this: clamp a square at the center of one top piece; lay a 2x4 in place with its top edge even with the top edge of the top piece end and the opposite end of the 2x4 at 10 inches on the carpenter's square. Mark for the cuts, and then make the cuts with a portable circular saw or saber saw **(Photo 6)**.

Anchor the rafters to the top edge of the top board with deck screws **(Photo 7)**. Then anchor them together at their peak with screws. Again predrill all holes. Cut the corner braces for the top, and anchor them in place **(Photo 8)**. Add a temporary brace at the bottom; then turn the assembly over, and install the back top board and rafters.

Rip the roof cross-pieces, and cut them to length; then fasten them in place with galvanized or stainless-steel nails **(Photo 9)**. Add a second temporary brace at the bottom, and you're ready to move the arbor out of your shop, garage, or other work area and anchor it in place.

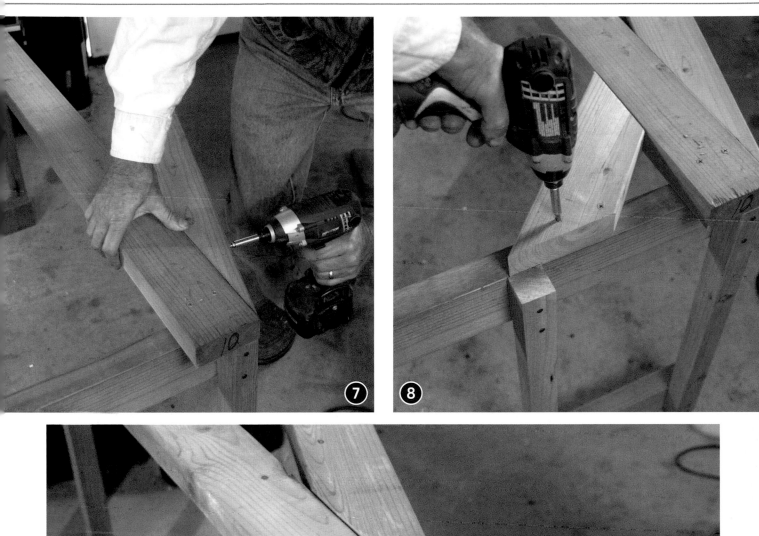

Potting Cart

Time to Complete: 3-4 Hours

Potting is usually a seasonal thing. In the spring, you pot plants for the garden, deck, or flower bed. In the fall, perhaps you're digging up perennials, dividing, and repotting for the next year. In any case, a potting cart can make the chores easier, holding all the materials and tools needed from one season to the next. The cart shown not only holds a lot, but because it's on wheels, you can move it into the garage or garden shed, and back out as needed. And the cart also has a built-in "faucet" for easy watering of your potted plants. Like many projects in this book, the potting cart is made of pressure-treated lumber for long-lasting outdoor use.

POTTING CART

Shopping List:

3 Pressure-treated 2x4, 12' long

1 Pressure-treated 2x4, 8' long

2 Pressure-treated ¾x6 decking boards, 12' long

2 Wheels

Axle, ½" threaded rod x 36", cut to fit

2 Locknuts and washers, ½"

1 PVC pipe, 1" x 36"

2 PVC L-fittings, 1"

1 PVC hose connector, 1"

1 PVC shutoff, 1"

Plumber's strapping, 6"

6d galvanized nails

Cutting List:

4 End frame, top & bottom, 1½" x 3½" x 17"

4 Side frame, top & bottom, 1½" x 3½" x 32"

2 Front legs, 1½" x 3½" x 30"

2 Back legs, 1½" x 3½" x 28"

6 Shelf boards, 1½" x 3½" x 20"

2 Handles, 1½" x 3½" x 12"

4 Top, 1" x 5½" x 36"

2 End skirt boards, 1" x 5½" x 20½"

1 Back skirt boards, 1" x 5½" x 38"

Potting Cart

Turn a locking nut on one end of the threaded rod; then add a pair of washers on one wheel. Tap the rod through one hole in the lower horizontals, then into the opposite hole (**Photo 4**). Add another pair of washers and another wheel, and then turn on the other locking nut to secure both wheels (**Photo 5**).

Turn the assembly right-side up. Fasten the bottom boards in place with 3-inch deck screws, spacing them evenly apart (**Photo 6**).

Fasten the top boards in place with 3-inch deck screws (**Photo 7**).

place to the bottom edge of the backboards and to the end skirt boards (Photo 11).

Enlarge the squared drawing for the handles, and cut them to shape using a saber saw (Drawing A).

Fasten the handles in place using 3-inch deck screws (Photo 12).

Assemble the faucet as shown in the drawing. Cut all pieces to length; smooth their ends; and use plastic pipe cement to fasten them together. Fasten the assembly to the back of the potting cart with plumber's strapping (Drawing B).

1" SQUARES Ⓐ

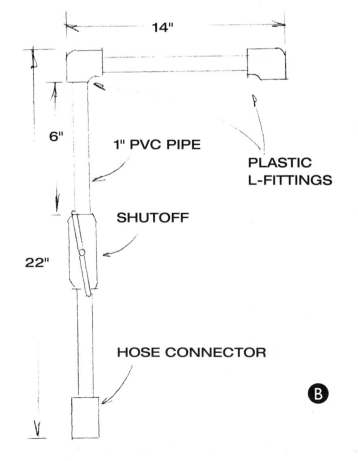

14"

6"   1" PVC PIPE

PLASTIC L-FITTINGS

SHUTOFF

22"

HOSE CONNECTOR Ⓑ

Cut the end skirt boards to size, including their rounded front edges (Photo 8). Use a bucket or similar round item or a compass to determine the shape, and cut out using a saber saw (Photo 9).

Fasten the end skirt boards to the bottom edges of the top boards with 6d galvanized nails. You will probably have to predrill with a ⅛-inch bit to prevent splitting the stock on the ends (Photo 10). Then fasten the back skirt board in

Compost Bin

Composting is a great way of recycling yard and garden debris such as leaves, small branches, pulled end-of-the-year garden and flower plants, as well as grass clippings and even some table scraps. Not only does composting help solve the problem of today's overflowing landfills, but it beats bagging and carrying lawn and garden debris to the curb side. The compost bin shown is quite simple to make using pressure-treated materials. The framework is of 2x4s, and the sides from $^5/_4$x6 decking. A front door is hinged for easy access when cleaning out the bin or turning the materials. The bin is assembled using 6d galvanized nails.

COMPOST BIN

Shopping List:

6 pressure-treated $^5/_4$x6s, 12' long

1 pressure-treated 2x4, 12' long

1 pressure-treated 2x4, 8' long

Galvanized 6d nails

2 hinges, 3" strap

2 hooks and screw eyes, 3"

Cutting List:

6 upright braces: 1½" x 3½" x 33½"

24 side pieces, 1" x 5½" x 36"

Compost Bin

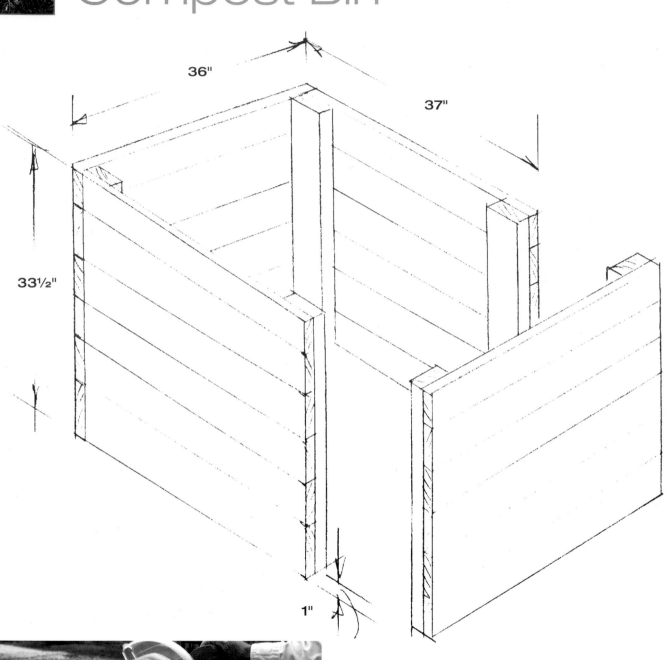

36"

37"

33½"

1"

①

Note that the door is made in the same manner as the sides, but it is set up 1 inch from the bottom to allow for easy opening **(drawing)**.

The first step is to cut the upright 2×4 supports and horizontal side pieces to length **(Photo 1)**. Place the pieces on a worktable or sawhorses, and fasten the side pieces to the end uprights using 6d galvanized nails **(Photo 2)**.

Drive one nail; then make sure the first side pieces are square with the uprights by checking with a carpenter's square **(Photo 3)**. Then continue nailing the sides to the uprights.

USING YOUR COMPOST BIN

Properly used, your compost bin will produce compost from your yard and garden "waste." Most of the weed seeds and insects will be killed by the composting action in the bin.

When you clean your yard and garden in the fall, first place materials in separate piles. This includes piles of leaves, twigs and sticks, and the like.

If you can't use the piles immediately, cover them with tarps. You will also need green materials, such as grass clippings, and some top soil. Once you have the materials on hand, begin by layering them into the bin. Start with a loose layer of materials such as twigs or leaves. Then add a layer of topsoil and a bit of natural fertilizer such as rotted manure. Grass clippings and kitchen scraps, such as vegetable peelings and fruit pieces, can also be added to help speed the decomposition of the materials. Do not add any meat scraps.

Continue layering with a layer of lighter materials, followed by the denser layers, until the bin is full. Then cover the bin with a piece of black plastic or plastic tarp, and weight the tarp down so it can't blow off.

In a couple of weeks you should turn the pile with a pitch fork and then continue to turn it weekly. After about another month, the compost should be ready to use.

Stand the two completed sides upright. (You may need a helper.) Fasten the bottom "back" board in place, again making sure the assembly is square (**Photo 4**).

Temporarily fasten the top back board in place to hold the assembly (**Photo 5**). Then continue nailing the back boards in place. When you reach the top board, temporarily tack it in place; realign if needed; then fasten in place as well.

Construct the front door, and hinge it in place (**Photo 6**). It should sit up from the bottom about 1 inch to allow for easy opening. Install the metal hooks and screw eyes on the opposite side from the hinges to hold the front closed.

Time to Complete: 3-4 Hours

Pergola

A pergola can add beauty to your yard, deck, or even patio. It can also establish the decor of your outdoor living area, or be used as an inviting entryway, such as the California redwood pergola shown, coupled with a privacy fence and a wrought iron gate. And the pergola shown is quite easily made, using stock materials. Incidentally, this is another project you may wish to pre-finish before assembling. Deck stain or finish is the best choice.

PERGOLA

Shopping List:

2 6x6 Posts, 10' long

4 2x6, 8' long

4 Bags concrete mix

1½" deck screws

3" deck screws

Cutting List:

2 Posts, 5½" x 5½" x 10'

4 Lower cross supports, 1½" x 5½" x 24"

2 Upper cross supports, 1½" x 5½" x 66"

8 Top pieces, 1½" x 1½" x 24"

Pergola

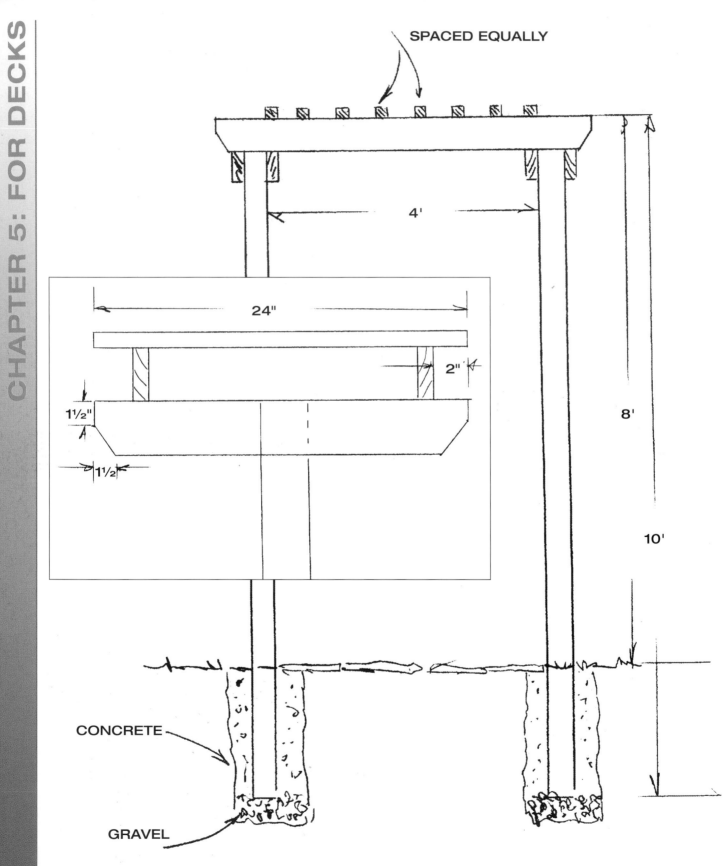

SPACED EQUALLY

4'

24"

2"

1½"

1½

8'

10'

CONCRETE

GRAVEL

The pergola is supported by posts set in concrete. Dig the holes, and add gravel or rocks to the bottom to help support the posts and provide drainage. Then set the posts, and pour concrete around them **(Drawings)**. Make sure the posts are set the correct distance apart and that they are plumb in both directions and level across their tops. Use a level to determine plumb and level; then install temporary braces to hold the posts upright until the concrete sets **(Photo 1)**.

Cut the lower cross supports to length, and cut their decorative ends. Then fasten to the posts with 3-inch deck screws. Make sure they are level **(Photo 2)**. Cut the upper cross supports to length, and cut their decorative ends as well. Then anchor them in place on top of the bottom cross supports with 1½-inch deck screws driven at an angle **(Photo 3)**.

Rip the top pieces to width, and cut to length; then anchor them to the top edges of the upper cross supports, spacing them equally **(Photo 4)**.

Time to Complete: 2-3 Hours

Classic Redwood Side Table

A small table that perfectly matches the classic redwood picnic table is a welcome addition to a deck, patio, or yard. This deck table can be made with the end pieces left from the Classic Redwood Picnic Table. Use the end pieces left from the 8-foot 2x6s and some 2x4 scraps. The small table is easily constructed using the same basic construction methods as the picnic table. You may wish to make several of these handy, easy-to-make tables.

CLASSIC REDWOOD TABLE

Shopping List:

1 Redwood 2x6, 8' long

1 Redwood 2x4, 10' long

2½" deck screws

Cutting List:

3 Top, 1½" x 5½" x 17"

2 Ends, 1½" x 3½" x 15"

2 Sides, 1½" x 3½" x 12"

4 Legs, 1½" x 3½" x 16½"

Classic Redwood Side Table

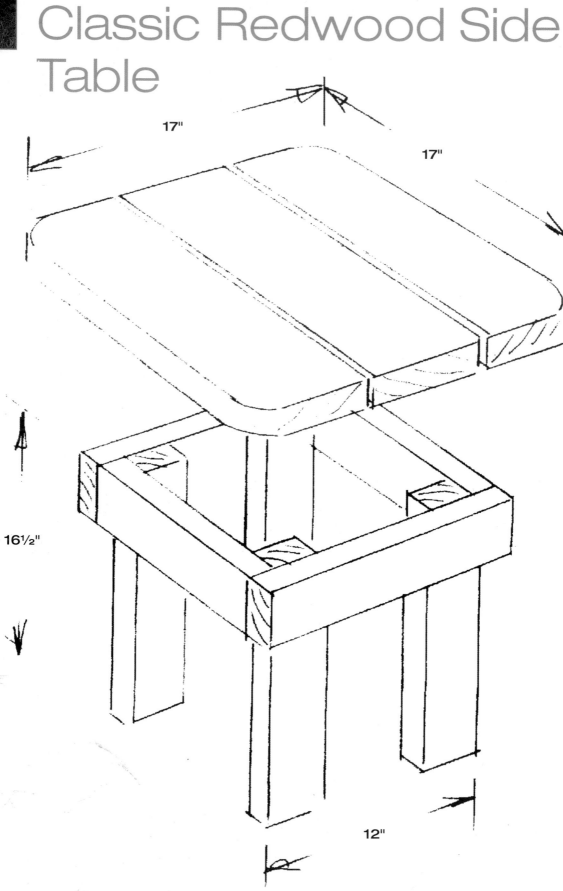

17"

17"

16½"

12"

Round the ends of the two outside top boards using a saber saw **(Photo 5)**. Then space the top boards in the same manner as for the picnic tabletop, and attach them to the framework through the countersunk holes in the underside framework **(Photo 6)**.

Stand the table upright, and sand or finish as needed **(Photo 7)**.

Cut the ends, sides, and legs from redwood 2×4 scrap pieces. Attach one side piece to the top of two legs by first predrilling the holes **(Photo 1)**. Then fasten the two legs with 2½-inch deck screws **(Photo 2)**. Attach the other side piece to the two remaining legs in the same manner.

Now bore the underside framing members of the two end pieces with countersunk holes for attaching the top to the table framework with wood screws **(Photo 3)**. Then attach the assembled end pieces to the sides by predrilling, making sure the framework is square and then attaching with 2½-inch deck screws through the framework and into the legs **(Photo 4)**.

Time to Complete: 3-4 Hours

Deck Cushion Storage Locker

Storing chair and lounge cushions during the off-season can be a hassle. These things take up lots of space. If you have a raised deck, an excellent solution is to build an under-deck seat cushion storage area or locker. You'll need to make the storage area watertight, as well as sealed so wasps and other insects and pests can't get in. The storage locker shown is made of ½-inch pressure-treated plywood and pressure-treated 2x2 and 2x4 framing. The 2x2s are used as strengtheners and as glue blocks. Like aircraft and wooden boat construction, this cuts down on weight but provides a sturdy construction. Use waterproof glue, and check that all fasteners are deck screws suitable for use with pressure-treated materials.

DECK CUSHION STORAGE LOCKER

Shopping List:

3 Sheets ¾" pressure-treated plywood

2 Pressure-treated 2x4, 8' long

2 Pressure-treated 2x4, 10' long

3 Pressure-treated ⅝x6, 8' long

2 Concrete blocks or deck piers

1 Pair hinges

1 Door latch

Cutting List:

3 Sides and top, ¾" plywood, 38" x 38" (cut to fit)

2 Back and bottom, ¾" plywood, 36" x 36"

2 Base frame front and back, 1½" x 3½" x 36"

3 Base frame sides and center, 1½" x 3½" x 33"

2 Top frame front and back, 1½" x 1½" x 36"

3 Top frame sides and center, 1½" x 1½" x 33"

4 Vertical glue strip stiffeners, 1½" x 1½" x 31"

4 Door uprights, 1" x 5½" x 40" or to match deck height

2 Door supports, 1" x 5½" x 40" or to match deck height

2 Door cross braces, 1" x 5½" x 18"

Deck Cushion Storage Locker

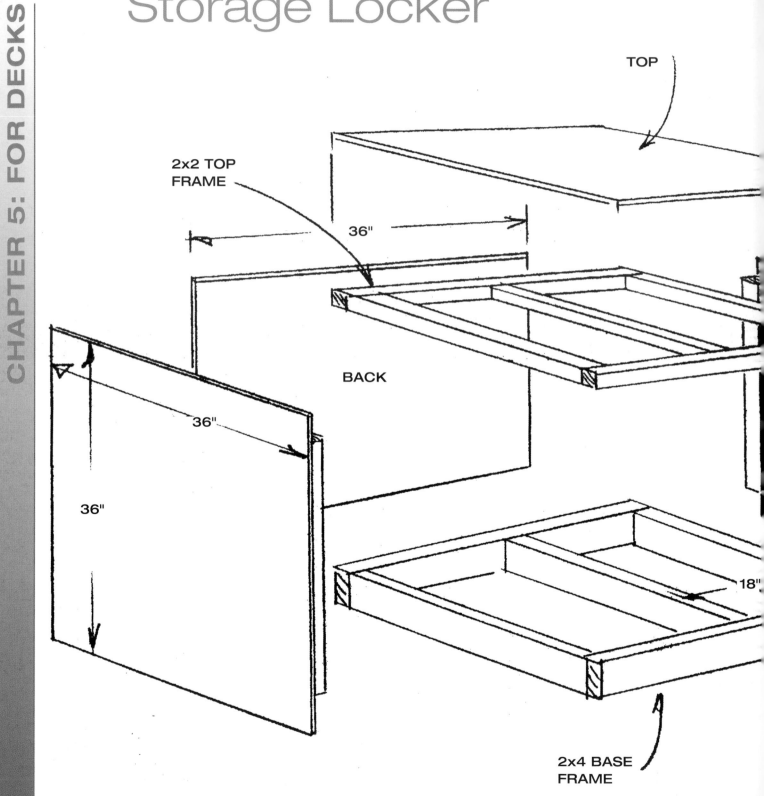

TOP

2x2 TOP
FRAME

36"

BACK

36"

36"

36"

18"

2x4 BASE
FRAME

The locker is basically a wooden box anchored to the deck posts or other supports and further supported at the back by concrete deck blocks. You will probably have to change the dimensions of the storage box to suit your deck height. The box can be almost any size, as long as there is adequate storage room for your needs **(Drawing)**.

The first step is to cut the plywood pieces to size **(Photo 1)**. Rip a pressure-treated 2x4 to create the 2x2 glue strips, and cut the glue strips and the top frame pieces to length. Fasten the glue strips to the plywood edges of the sides using waterproof glue and deck screws **(Photo 2)**.

SIDE

2x2 STIFFENERS

Cut the bottom frame from 2x4s, and assemble with glue and deck screws **(Photo 3)**. Fasten the sides to the bottom frame using glue and deck screws. Fasten the back to the glue strips on the sides. Fasten the bottom in place. Assemble the top frame, and fasten down on top of the glue strips with screws from the sides and back into the top frame. Install the bottom and top using waterproof glue and deck screws **(Photo 4)**.

Deck Cushion Storage Locker ❖ 125

Deck Cushion Storage Locker

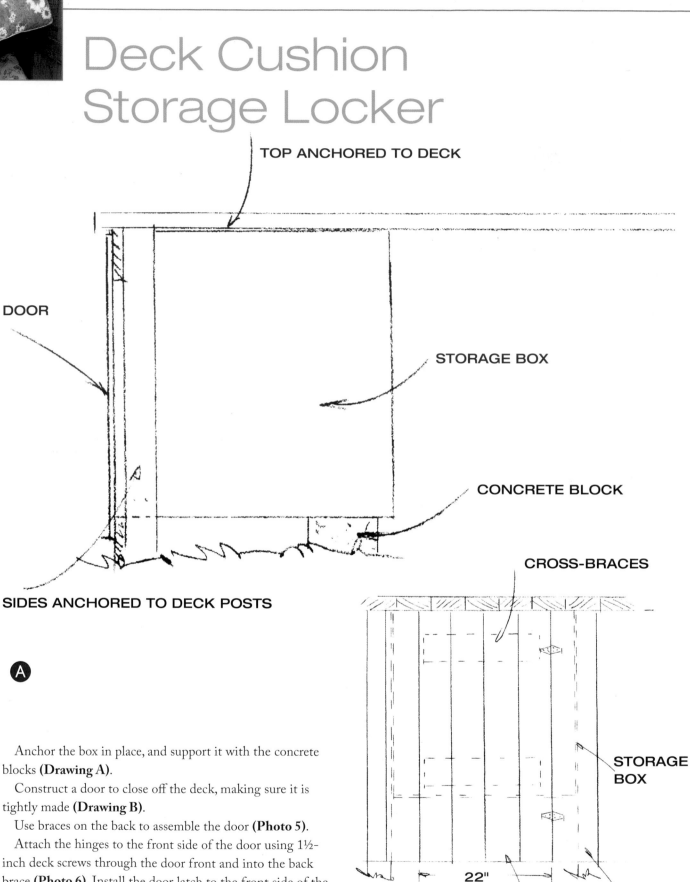

TOP ANCHORED TO DECK

DOOR

STORAGE BOX

CONCRETE BLOCK

CROSS-BRACES

SIDES ANCHORED TO DECK POSTS

A

STORAGE BOX

22"

B

DECK POSTS

Anchor the box in place, and support it with the concrete blocks (**Drawing A**).

Construct a door to close off the deck, making sure it is tightly made (**Drawing B**).

Use braces on the back to assemble the door (**Photo 5**).

Attach the hinges to the front side of the door using 1½-inch deck screws through the door front and into the back brace (**Photo 6**). Install the door latch to the front side of the door in the same manner (**Photo 7**). Then fasten the door in place with hinges (**Photo 8**).

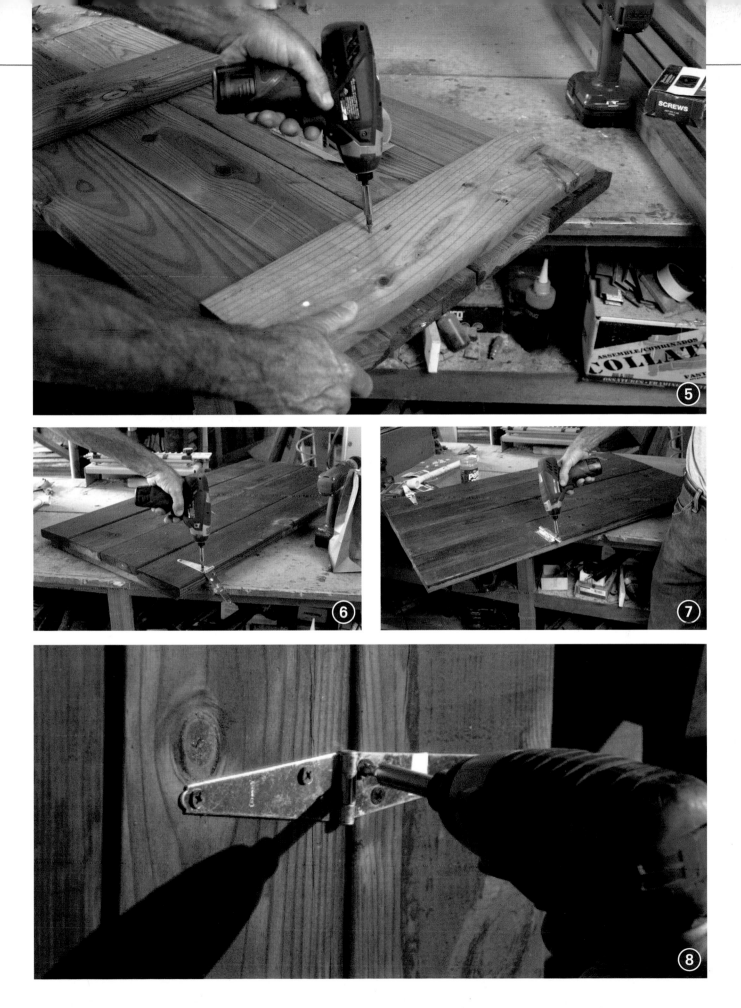

Planter Bench

Time to Complete: 5-6 Hours

Some of the best outdoor furniture combines more than one purpose into a single piece. This planter bench does that nicely, offering a place to display your plants year-round as well as seating for your backyard. This piece would also make a good addition to a patio or deck. Slightly altered, it could even be transformed into a handy storage bench to hide clutter and useful but unattractive supplies that would otherwise interfere with your streamlined, garden-beautiful look. In fact, the storage bench project presented in the first section of this book is a variation on this design. As a bonus, just as with raised-bed gardening, plants are much easier to tend without all that stooping down, making for thriving plants and a happy back.

PLANTER BENCH
Shopping List:
8 2x4, 10 feet long
2½" galvanized screws
2½" galvanized finishing nails
Waterproof glue
Stain or paint
Cutting List:
3 1½" x 3½" x 48" Seat boards
2 1½" x 3½" x 11" Seat braces
24 1½" x 3½" x 18" Vertical sides
16 1½" x 3½" x 9½" Internal box cleats
2 1½" x 3½" x 11" Hanger brace
8 1½" x 3½" x 12" Frame sides

Planter Bench

Apply some glue under the ends of the center seat board. Still using that ¼-inch drill bit as a spacer to maintain the correct gap, drill a pair of pilot holes as before **(Photo 10)**. Drive in the screws, and remove all the clamps. The seat assembly is complete **(Photo 11)**.

Each side of the two planter boxes is made with five components—three vertical 18-inch lengths of 2x4 and a pair of 9½-inch lengths that function as cleats to hold the side assembly together from the inside. Because each of the completed sides is attached to the next in an interlocking fashion, the internal cleats must be offset by the thickness of

your worktable **(Photo 5)**. Use a square to be sure the assembly didn't accidentally shift out-of-square while flipping it over. Because the glue has not yet set, you can easily adjust the assembly back into square. Replace the middle board, and line it up so the gaps are of equal size. The design calls for a gap of ¼-inch, so note how a ¼-inch drill bit makes a handy gauge to set the distance between the boards.

You'll need to drill some pilot holes for the 2½-inch galvanized screws used to attach the seat to the braces. Use a screw as a gauge to select a drill bit of the correct size **(Photo 6)**. Drill a pair of pilot holes in each of the outer boards, one to either side of the clamp **(Photo 7)**, and drive the screws home to secure the boards to the support brace.

Now is a good time to mark and cut the matching hanger braces for the planter boxes. Slip a length of 2x4 into the end space **(Photo 8)**, and mark with a pencil; then cut the hanger brace on a miter saw **(Photo 9)**. Put the hanger braces aside for now.

a 2x4 to allow the edge of each subsequent side to nest into the corner. To be sure the offset is correct, test-fit each side for the correct offset using a length of 2x4 scrap as a spacer **(Photo 12)**, and adjust the length of the internal cleat so it is flush with the opposite edge.

As before, put glue on the outer pieces where the cleats make contact; then drill pilot holes and drive a pair of screws to secure the cleats into place top and bottom **(Photo 13, next page)**. With the two outer boards attached, remove the spacer; then repeat the process with the center board. A ¼-inch drill bit laid on the worktable and inserted into the gap from the ends will help maintain spacing. Assemble the remaining three sides of the planter box in the same manner.

Planter Bench

Fit the corner of a pair of box sides together, and you'll see how they nestle in the crook created by the offset internal cleat **(Photo 14)**. Although only miter cuts and simple butt joints are used for the assembly of the projects throughout this book, this L-shaped crook functions as a joint called a rabbet. The mating pieces touch on two sides, which not only adds strength to the joint but works to keep the corner joint square.

Apply some glue to the mating surfaces of the corners, and then drive piloted screws from the outside to secure the corners top and bottom **(Photo 15)**. Do this with all four corners in turn; then repeat the entire process to construct the other planter box. Attach the frame sides, making sure that the corners meet at the proper angle so that they don't gap **(Photo 16)**. Attach the hanger cleat you cut earlier to the inside face of the planter boxes, securing it just below the edge of the top frame **(Photo 17)**.

Set the completed seat assembly onto the hanger braces on the planter boxes—a little trial and error may be necessary to the get the boxes the right distance apart, so this might

be a good time to enlist the help of a second person to take care of one end while you take care of the other **(Photo 18)**. The seat should make a perfect fit as the two braces on the underside of the seat meet face-to-face. Drill pilot holes through the braces, and attach the seat assembly to the boxes with screws, but don't drive the screws quite all the way in yet. You want the seat secure for the next step, but you'll then disassemble it for staining or painting.

Sand all faces smooth, paying particular attention to any components that meet flush, such as where the ends of the seat assembly meet the sides of the top frame on the boxes **(Photo 19)**. The edges of commercial 2x4s are already rounded, but run the sander over each edge and over every corner to eliminate any sharp spots.

For final finishing, back the screws out of the seat mounting braces and remove the seat assembly. Staining or painting the three components of the planter bench separately is not only easier but ensures that every wood surface is covered to help protect it from the weather **(Photo 20)**. And if you constructed your bench in a garage or basement shop, it will be a lot easier to move the unit around dismantled. The bench can be reassembled in its final location.

No-Raccoon Trash-Can Locker

Time to Complete: 3-4 Hours

If varmints such as raccoons, or even the neighborhood dogs and cats, make regular forays into your trash, you might consider this heavy-duty locker. The locker can also do double duty as a pet-food locker, using the trash can inside the locker to hold the pet food. The no-raccoon locker features a lift-up lid for placing trash into the can inside, and a front door for removing or placing the trash can into the locker. A drop bolt on the front door keeps the locker securely closed. The locker shown, made entirely of pressure-treated 2x4 and ⁵⁄₄-by lumber, will be long lasting. The pressure-treated lumber also offers another advantage over standard pine construction lumber in that it's fairly weighty, so the locker is heavy and not easily tipped or turned over by pets or varmints.

NO-RACCOON TRASH CAN LOCKER

Shopping List:

6 2x4, 8' long

10 ⁵⁄₄x6, 8' long

2 3" strap hinges

2 4" butt hinges

Drop-bolt catch

8d galvanized nails

Cutting List:

4 Bottom framework pieces
   1½" x 3½" x 23¾"

4 Top framework pieces,
   1½" x 3½" x 23¾"

7 Floor boards, 1½" x 3½" x 23¾"

12 Side and end uprights,
   1" x 5½", 40" long

4 Lid boards, 1" x 5½" x 30" long

2 Lid board braces,
   1½" x 3½" x 20½"

1 Door holding strip, 1" x 1½",
   38" long

4 Door Boards, 1" x 5½", 38" long

2 Door braces, 1½" x 3½" x 22¾"

No-Raccoon
Trash-Can Locker

FRONT VIEW

DOOR

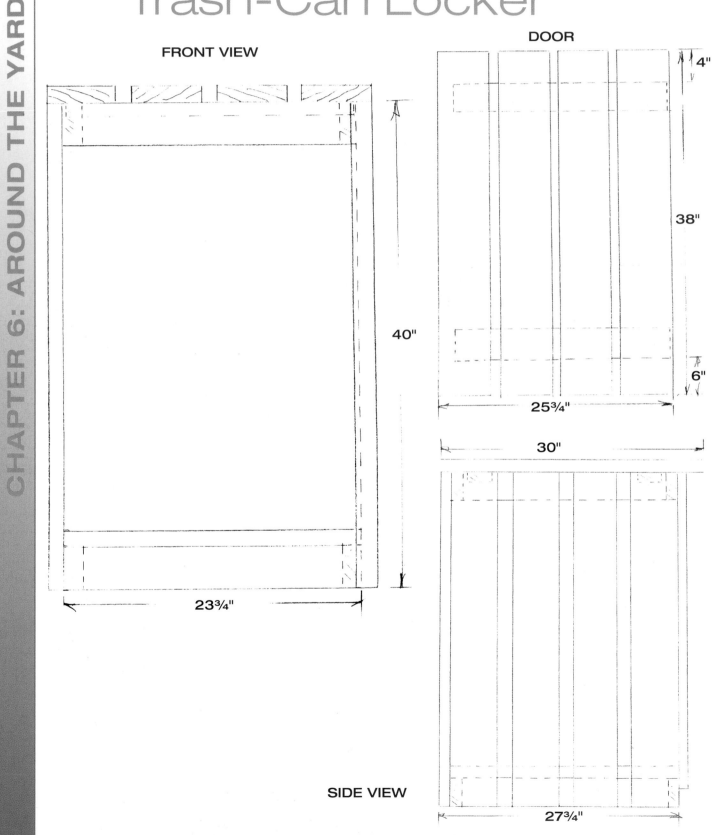

4"

38"

40"

6"

25¾"

30"

23¾"

SIDE VIEW

27¾"

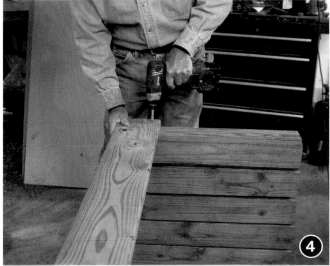

The locker shown is designed to fit a 32-gallon trash container. If you have a different size trash container, merely adjust the inside size to fit, making the locker at least 2 inches bigger all around **(Drawings)**.

The first step is to cut all pieces to the correct length following the cutting list **(Photo 1)**. The locker assembles easily. Use 3-inch deck screws to construct the bottom base framework. Make sure the frame is assembled square, checking it with a carpenter's square **(Photo 2)**. Fasten the 2x4 floor on the base framework using galvanized 8d nails. Position a floor board on each side of the framework, and fasten it in place. Then space the remaining pieces between, creating equal spaces **(Photo 3)**. Assemble the top frame in the same manner, and then stand the frames upright on a smooth, flat surface, such as a shop or garage floor. Fasten one upright piece in place at one side of the frames with one screw in each end **(Photo 4)**. Make sure the assembly is square **(Photo 5)**. And then drive a second screw into each end of each side piece **(Photo 6)**.

No-Raccoon Trash Can Locker

Fasten the remaining side pieces in place, spacing them equally apart. Repeat for the opposite side and back **(Photo 7)**. With the basic locker framed in, turn it up on its bottom and construct the lid on the open top. Begin construction with the lid upside down. Lay the lid pieces across the top; cut the cross-braces; and drive a 2-inch deck screw down through the braces into the lid pieces. This will temporarily hold them in place **(Photo 8)**. Turn the lid upright, and drive two screws down through each lid piece into both cross-braces **(Photo 9)**.

With the assembled lid in place, fasten it to the locker using hinges. Use 1-inch screws rather than the short screws that typically come with a package of hinges. Note because you are driving into the end grain, strap hinges bent down over the top can add strength **(Photo 10)**. Rip a strip for the front-door anchor strip, and fasten in place with screws **(Photo 11)**.

Assemble the door, making sure the assembly is square **(Photo 12)**. Then fasten the door in place with butt hinges, and install the drop-latch **(Photo 13)**.

Resources

Other Recommended Reading

Backyard Structures and How to Build Them
by Monte Burch
Step-by-step instructions show you how to build projects that include a birdhouse and one-stall horse stable. (Outdoor World Press, Inc.)

Cabinets, Shelves & Home Storage Solutions
by the Editors of Creative Homeowner
Utilize the space you have by creating functional storage units. This book includes instructions and illustrations for dozens of projects that can help you tidy up any room in the house. (Creative Homeowner)

The Complete Manual of Woodworking
by Albert Jackson
This book will not only teach you all you need to know about woodworking, but it will also inspire you to new carpentering heights. (Alfred A. Knopf)

Design Ideas for Decks & Patios
by the Editors of Creative Homeowner
Portfolios of lavish photographs and an easy-to-understand design section guides readers through the basics of the planning process and provides ideas and inspiration. (Creative Homeowner)

Dictionary of Woodworking Tools
by R. A. Salaman
Before you can be a cooper or a wheelwright, you have to know your rasp from your fretsaw. (Atragal Press)

Furniture Projects for the Deck and Lawn: Attractive 2x4 Woodworking Projects Anyone Can Build
by John Kelsey and Ian J. Kirby
If you can't get enough of outdoor projects, check out this book, which shows how to make projects ranging from a bird feeder, a wooden swing, an umbrella table, and planter boxes to a play house. (Cambrium Press)

Green Woodworking Pattern Book: Over 300 Traditional Craft Designs
by Ray Tabor
Create hundreds of useful projects without harming the Earth. (Batsford Books)

Hand Tool Essentials: Refine Your Power Tool Projects with Hand Tool Techniques
by Popular Woodworking Editors
Before the days of power tools, carpenters relied on simple shop tools and skilled hands—and you can, too. (Popular Woodworking Books)

Home Woodworking Projects: Beautiful & Functional Items for Every Room
by Shady Oak Press
Instead of just learning how to build it, learn how to build it to last. Includes 24 step-by-step practical projects. (Shady Oak Press)

The Kids' Building Workshop: 15 Woodworking Projects for Kids and Parents to Build Together
by Craig Robertson
Get your little aspiring carpenters off on the right foot. Whether you're passing on the trade or are new to the world of wood yourself, the methods taught in this title are designed to be easy to pick up for you and your youngster. (Storey Publishing, LLC)

Tool School: The Missing Manual for Your Tools
by Monte Burch
Take the guesswork out of buying and using new tools. Recommended for beginning and intermediate woodworkers. (Popular Woodworking Books)

Toys, Games, and Furniture: Over 30 Woodworking Projects You Can Make for Children
by Family Handyman Magazine Editors
With the help of this book, you will be able to give even Santa and his elves a run for their money. (Reader's Digest)

Other Recommended Reading (continued)

Ultimate Guide to Barns, Shreds, and Outbuildings
by John D. Wagner
This book provides everything you need to know to improve your property by adding a new barn or outbuilding. You will find a mix of design inspiration and practical information to help you complete your project. (Creative Homeowner)

Ultimate Guide to Decks
by Steve Cory
You'll find the information you need to build the deck of your dreams. Comprehensive instructions show you how to build like a pro. (Creative Homeowner)

Ultimate Guide to Fences, Gates, and Trellises
by Editors of Creative Homeowner
Whether you're looking to keep critters in or out of your yard or you just want to give your home the perfect decorative accent, this guide has what you need to get the job done. Various types of gates include pickets, split-rails, board designs, and more. (Creative Homeowner)

Ultimate Guide to Gazebos & Other Outdoor Structures
by the Editors of Creative Homeowner
Enrich any outdoor space while also creating a place where you can enjoy the sounds and smells of an afternoon rain shower. Picking the right spot, using right materials and customizing it to your taste and style—it's all covered right here. (Creative Homeowner)

Ultimate Guide to House Framing
by John D. Wagner
Build a house—or almost any structure—from the ground up. This book gives you the tools you will need to construct a safe and stable structure. From choosing the proper lumber to learning how to read a blueprint all the way to hammering that last nail into the roof. (Creative Homeowner)

Ultimate Guide to Kids' Play Structures and Tree Houses
by Jeff Beneke and Steve Willson
Detailed plans and step-by-step instructions to make 10 structures, with designs conforming to guidelines of the U.S. Consumer Product Safety Commission. (Creative Homeowner)

Ultimate Guide to Yard and Garden Sheds
by John D. Wagner
The book shows you how to pick the right type of shed and site it in the appropriate place. Photos provide step-by-step instruction for construction of different popular styles. (Creative Homeowner)

Woodworking for Dummies
by Jeff Strong
Intimidated by the idea of using tools on wood but have a yen to try it? This book might help you overcome your jitters so you can make some sawdust fly. (Wiley Publishing)

SOME SHOPPING OPTIONS

Ace Hardware
http://www.acehardware.com

Benjamin Moore
http://www.benjaminmoore.com

Craftman/Sears
http://www.craftman.com

Do It Best
http://doitbest.com

Expo
http://www.expo.com

Home Depot
http://www.homedepot.com

Lowes
http://www.lowes.com

Glossary

A

air-dried wood Wood that is dried naturally.

angle square An isosceles triangle–shaped measuring device; also known by the brand name Speed Square.

B

bar clamp A C-shaped device with a sliding jaw used to temporarily secure two or more objects; *see also* C-clamp.

belt sander A powered sander using a rotating belt to smooth wood surfacing.

bevel An angle other than a right angle cut into wood *with* the grain.

biscuit A small wafer of pressed wood used to fuse two pieces of wood together; *see also* dowel.

bolt A threaded rod with a head used with a nut to secure an item.

bore To create a hole in an object.

C

C-clamp C-shaped device used to temporarily secure two or more objects.

carpenter's square An L-shaped tool used to create right angles.

casters Wheels that attach to the bottom of a piece of furniture, enabling it to move with greater ease.

cedar A type of tree that bears durable lumber as well as an attractive grain and scent; *see also* red cedar.

circular saw An electric-powered portable saw with a circular blade.

cleat A brace used to help support a structure.

compass Device that helps to create a perfect circle.

countersink A screw inserted below the surface of the object it enters.

crosscut A cut made across the grain of the wood instead of with it.

cross lap A lap joint that consists of two objects overlapped in their centers, creating an X-shape.

D

deck screws Specially crafted screws manufactured to resist corrosion and to start with ease.

dowel A short peg of wood used to fuse two pieces of wood together.

drill press A stationary drilling machine.

drive To move or propel with force.

F

fastener A hardware component—such as a nail, screw, staple, or bolt—that joins two pieces together.

finish A final coat of varnish or sealant applied to wood at the completion of a project.

flange A projecting rim used for support, or in fixing one object to another.

Forstner bit A precision drilling bit capable of drilling smooth, flat-bottom holes.

finishing hammer A small 12-ounce hammer for driving finishing nails without marring the wood surface.

framing hammer A straight, clawed heavy-duty rip hammer.

G

galvanized Describes a coating of zinc added to nails and screws to prevent corrosion.

grain The direction and pattern of wood fibers in a piece of lumber.

grout A thin mortar used to fill in gaps or crevices in masonry.

H

hacksaw A fine-toothed handsaw set in a fixed frame used for cutting metal; also known as a metal saw.

header A crossbeam placed perpendicular to joists and flush with outer surface.

Glossary

hinge A jointed device that allows for movement of a door, lid, or other attached part.

I

impact driver A portable electric tool dedicated to driving screws.

J

jigsaw A power saw with a narrow reciprocating blade used to cut intricate curved detail; *see also* saber saw

joint The connection point between two pieces of wood, often joined by screws, nails, or glue.

joist Horizontal supporting beams that form the under-structure for a ceiling or floor.

K

knot The hard, dark cross-grained place on a piece of wood where a branch has grown. Also called a node.

kiln-dried wood Wood that is dried in a kiln rather than naturally; *see also* air-dried wood.

L

lag screw A thick wood screw with a hexagon-shaped head.

lag bolt A thick machine bolt with a hexagon-shaped head.

ledger board A support board anchored to a building to support a deck and other framing.

level A term that describes a horizontal surface with all points at the same elevation; a device used to determine whether a surface is level and/or plumb.

M

machine bolt Used to connect metal parts, this square- or hex-headed, threaded-shaft fastener can be tightened with a wrench.

miter An angle other than a right angle cut into wood *across* the grain.

miter box An open-ended box that guides handsaws in making crosscuts or miter cuts with fixed or changeable guides.

miter joint Two pieces of wood that meet at an angle, such as the corner of a wooden frame.

N

nail, common A nail with a large round head, used for framing where appearance is not important.

nail, finishing Nail with a smaller head, more frequently used for fine woodworking, where nails need to be inconspicuous.

notch A U- or V-shaped cut.

nut A short metal block, typically square or hexagonal, with a threaded center hole that fits on a bolt.

O

off-the-shelf lumber Standard dimension lumber.

orbital sander A powered sander that moves in an orbital pattern.

P

plumb Describes a structure or object that stands at 90 degrees, or straight up and down vertically.

plywood A panel made from thin layers of wood, also called plies or veneers, bonded together under pressure, with the grain of each layer running perpendicular to each other.

Glossary

power miter saw A powered saw used for crosscutting, including miters and bevels.

pressure-treated lumber Wood treated under high pressure and with preservatives; frequently used for outdoor projects.

protractor An instrument used to measure angles.

R

redwood A sturdy type of straight-grain wood favored by woodworkers for its durability, ease of use, and insect- and rot-resistance; has no pitch or resins and will readily take and retain paints and stains or weather naturally to a pleasant gray color.

red cedar The fragrant, long-lasting wood derived from cedar trees, often used in the construct of chests and closets; provides natural protection against moths.

ripping The process of cutting wood parallel with the grain.

router A powered tool used for cutting groove moldings and creating decorative edges.

S

sapwood The layer of a tree trunk between the bark and the heart that contains the sap.

slat A thin, narrow piece of material typically made of wood, stone, or metal.

splat A flat vertical support piece that is used for the backing on straight chairs.

saber saw A portable power saw with a reciprocating toothed blade used to cut curves; *see also* jigsaw.

sawhorse A four-legged support system usually used for resting wood being cut with a saw.

screed A tool with a straight edge used for smoothing concrete.

screw, wood A screw tapered to grip a piece of lumber as it enters the wood.

shim A small, tapered piece of material (often wood) used for making level adjustments or to fill space.

sheathing Plywood used as floor decking, house covering, or roof sheathing prior to the installation of finishing products such as flooring, siding, and shingles.

slurry A watery mixture of undissolved solids.

stain A tinted water-based or oil-based liquid used for coloring wood.

T

table saw A stationary or bench-top saw primarily used for ripping, but will also crosscut with a miter gauge.

trowel A small hand tool used in smoothing a finish on materials such as concrete or mortar.

W

warping The bending or twisting distortion of lumber when exposed to the elements.

washer A metal disc with a hole in the center used in conjunction with a nut or bolt to distribute pressure at the connection point.

weathering The process of natural aging of wood.

Index

Index

Credits and Acknowledgments

All photographs by Monte Burch except for those noted below:
Page 13 (top right and bottom left): © 2009, Jupiterimages, Incorporated
Page 70 (bottom right), page 113 (top right): Shutterstock/Tootles
Pages 128–29, 131 (top left, right column), 132–35, courtesy of Wayne Ellis
Pages 114–15: Photo courtesy of California Redwood Association/Tom Rider

About the Author

Monte Burch is an award-winning writer, photographer, and illustrator with thousands of magazine articles, photos, and illustrations to this credit. He is also the author of more than 70 books, including *The Home Cabinetmaker*, *The Complete Guide to Building Log Homes*, and *Tool School: The Missing Manual for Your Tools*. Burch lives in Missouri, and his Web site is www.monteburch.com.